Happiness Is A Warm Foxhole

S. Keith Kreitman

Happiness Is A Warm Foxhole

Memoirs of a Combat Medic

NoMoreBoxes LLC
San Jose, CA USA

Interior and cover layout: Thaddeus O. Cooper

Published by NoMoreBoxes LLC,
San Jose, CA 95128

S. KEITH KREITMAN

"When the snow is falling, the winds are howling, and the enemy is lurking, happiness is, indeed, a warm foxhole!"

PREFACE

This not a conventional war book.

It is not a chronological description of battle events.

If you are looking for adventurous "over the top" John Wayne hero action, this is not the place for it.

This is only a book about war's lessons upon only one person, myself, an eighteen-year-old Chicago-born son of European immigrant parents, a draftee during World War II.

As in life, generally, war is not all sad, it is not all humorous. It is just an expanded variation upon life's experiences.

You may be wondering why after almost sixty-two years I am even writing about a subject so heavily covered in the intervening years.

It is simply that before this, I never really believed that I was able to interpret my experience with enough clarity.

Now, after all these many years, I realize that I did understand it, and in fact it was a harbinger for so much that occurred to me and this country afterward.

Furthermore, less important events have now faded from memory, clearing the way for seminal influential events to remain in bold relief, like the tops of a range of mountains blanketed in clouds.

This is a book based only upon those images still vivid after all these years, as factual as memory and records may make them.

In order to be fair to all people I am writing about, no longer here to correct errors or defend themselves, I have changed all names and identifying unit designations.

THE KINETICS OF PITCHED CLOSE COMBAT

"Describing pitched close combat in mere words is impossible.

Because it is all encompassing, six dimensional, from the front, the left, the right, ricochets from the back, exploding shells from above and shaking ground from below.

It involves blurred vision from sweaty eyes, the acrid choking smell of layers of gunpowder smoke, ear-bursting horrible noises, the kinetic nerve vibrations from exploding mortars, hand grenades and shells, the screams of humans, the cries of the wounded, the piercing whine of ricochets of bullets and shrapnel, hiding behind or stepping over bodies of, perhaps, someone you know.

All at one time.

No media can ever duplicate it.

No words can fully convey it.

But once exposed to the heat of it, it welds one into a bonding, not only with friend, but foe, that no one else, no matter how close to you, will ever be able to share."

I wrote this tribute to the combat rifleman for Col. Dave Grossman of West Point, and it is now included in his required reading.

So this is what World War II combat riflemen -- citizen soldiers all -- faced. They marched and moved through fear daily, in order to serve their nation. A few broke down. A very few ran.

But on the whole, most served because they were asked to, and if they survived, many needed to return to the same repressive social, racial, and economic pecking orders from whence they had emerged.

Meanwhile, the untested barracks and marching field heroes reemerged from their shadows to shine again, in all their former spit and polish glory.

As for us, we had marched where it counted. We were ready to go home again.

Part I
Drafted

THE ADVENTURE BEGINS

I looked up at the old dirty gray building on Adams Street in Chicago.

It was one of the few times in my life I was on time.

"U. S. Army Induction Center," the sign read.

It was May, 1944. I was about to become a churning molecule in what was later to be called "The Good War!"

The infantry! Why in the hell was I going into the infantry instead of a nice military band? Me, one of the youngest professional symphony players in the United States?

I'll tell you why I was going into the infantry. It was because of that mean Sergeant who said: "If my son carries a gun, you can carry a gun, too!"

Then, I learned my first lesson in the U.S. Army. You don't argue with Sergeants. In fact, never argue with a corporal, or even a Pfc.

He listened respectfully as I ran through my resume, and then said, "You are right! I don't believe carrying a rifle is good enough for you. You need a job that is bigger...more challenging.

I am going to assign you to a 57 millimeter anti-tank gun. The next step is 105 millimeter howitzers. Do you want to try for that, or would you rather call it quits while you are ahead?"

I picked up my chips and left. I didn't even tell him what my mother told me to say to him: "Tell them that you're not healthy enough to be in the Army."

THE GRIEVING MADONNA

"They took you?" She cried. "How could they take you? You're skin and bones!"

"That's all they need these days, Mom!"

I found it very painful to disabuse my mother of her most cherished maternal burden, my fragile and precarious health.

She didn't really believe I was going, until I actually went down the back stairs on that chilly May morning.

Then, a wail arose that is still remembered by the residents of that West Side Chicago neighborhood to this day. They thought it was an air raid siren.

That seemed strange to me, because she was always poo-pooing the anxieties of those mothers whose sons were already serving. As a matter of fact, all of these boys were still state-side in offices, or like my brother at an airfield in North Carolina.

But now, she elevated herself to a level of anxiety that won her great status among the sisterhood of anxious mothers and became the role model which all strove to emulate.

To hasten her thrust to canonization, I became the only family member other than my regular Army cousin who actually did what soldiers are expected to do: Serve in combat.

HISTORY'S GREATEST MELTING POT GETS STIRRED

We arrived for anti-tank gun training at a camp near a tiny town in central Texas at the beginning of the hottest months of the year. I have heard it said that the Sahara Desert is preferable to central Texas in summer, and I don't dispute that.

We draftees were mostly from the "farm band," stretching down the middle of the U.S. from Minnesota to Arkansas, with a smattering of city boys, and the peppering of the inevitable "Boys from Brooklyn."

In that less traveled era, with no TV to illuminate the way, we were intimately interfaced for the first time with people of different heritages, national regions, and urban or rural cultures that we had only read about, if we were even capable of reading at all.

The proliferation of American-English dialects alone would have cast shadows over the tower of Babel. If I wanted to communicate with a Texan, I had to tell him that the cook wanted us to "warsh" the dishes and then "wrench" them clean.

Lord knows how they understood my high speed, Chicago Polish-molded dialect: "Hey, Stash! How about we go shoot some pool?"

THE BOYS IN THE BAND

The common thread in all new recruit units was the one or two who would put on an act of being (or in reality would be) mental cases trying like hell to be Army Section 8 out of the service.

Ours was a fellow by the name of Johnson, who defeated himself by being so systematically screwed up that the psychologists detected "method in his madness." He resolved that problem, eventually, by methodically shooting himself to death. My psychological nemesis was Workmacher, a German-American farm boy from Wisconsin, built like a bull, who bunked across from me.

Workmacher had no hand in the genes he inherited, nor did I. Had I been a Workmacher, the course of my life would most certainly have been different. I call it "physique determinism." Those favored by it take one path. Those who aren't take another. I took the other.

While he was out there being a football lineman and baseball slugger, I was usually the seventh man chosen on a pick-up baseball team of nine. While he busted balls tackling men, I busted fingers catching balls. Where he looked down at his victims, I looked up at my attackers.

When one is physically weak in the hostile world of teenagers, my type becomes a thinker, calculating how to survive the Workmachers. My assets were fast legs and a calculating mind.

Challenges to fist fights became ritualized like European duels. I would always show up with a second, to the surprise of the challenger, who did not expect me to show up at all.

Since I had the legs of a Fred Astaire and the movements of a Mohammed Ali to go with my Woody Allen punch, I danced about making my opponent mis-punch into a rage, usually screaming: "Stand still, you son-of-a-bitch!"

Then finally, and inevitably, he would land a bloody blow, at which point my second would break in and say: "You've had your pound of flesh!" and stop the action.

It was a win-win situation. He had satiated his blood lust and I had certified that I was not too chicken to show up.

Workmacher was the leader of what I came to call the "Farm Boy Machos." I was soon to discover that these were the first guys to collapse on hot, long marches, while their scrawny compatriots from the tough neighborhoods of Chicago, Brooklyn and Detroit stepped gingerly over them.

Then, there were Detroit and Lawson, with whom I later served in combat, and Minnesota, and acting corporal Peters, whom I will talk about later.

Riccarili was a street-wise Italian-American kid from Newark, New Jersey. He didn't want to be there and showed it. He had a body like Frank Sinatra and a similar warmth. He was someone you didn't want to screw around with. Except Schultz, one of the "farm boy machos," didn't know that.

One day, early on, some of us were in the company recreation room. I was reading in a chair, and I don't know what provoked it, but when Riccarili was passing him, Schultz grabbed his arm. It looked like a scene from "From Here To Eternity," where Frank Sinatra (playing Maggio) was being loomed over by Ernest Borgnine. By normal American standards, it was a mismatch: Bully Schultz picking on a shrimp.

Riccarili sort of slumped to the side and said in his inimitable Jersey accent, "Get out of my way, or I'll kick those balls you use for brains up into your head where they belong!"

Schultz looked dumfounded.

As a veteran of the Italian neighborhoods of Chicago, I jumped up and said, "He'll do it, Schultz! He'll do it!"

Schultz gave Riccarili another short push.

Riccarili did it!

Then he looked at me over the inert body of Schultz, who was now groaning in the fetal position on the floor, and winked.

East is East and Wisconsin is Wisconsin, and none of the farm-boy machos would ever pick on Riccarili again.

Finally, there was the usual assortment of non-memorable recruits: thieves, con artists and those who had to be thrown into the showers and fumigated for their lack of hygiene.

CORPORAL PUNISHMENT

Barracks sergeants varied. Ours was actually a corporal, returned to cadre duty in the U. S. because of an emotional breakdown in combat. Luckily he didn't emerge from his room at the end of the barracks very often, but when he did I avoided him as much as I was able.

Maluski was a Pole from Chicago, and if there is anything I knew about, it was Poles from Chicago.

To his credit he didn't specialize in bigotry. He hated all other groups, equally.

He hit the jackpot with Riccarili, whose distinction was bringing crabs into our platoon.

These, if you aren't familiar with them, are the little bugs that love to make their homes in pubic hair.

As soon as Maluski gave his first scratch, the order went out: "Shave! I don't want to see a single hair on balls twelve hours from now!"

Most recruits are pretty cowed, so there was a rush for the showers where Marquis de Sade would have been delighted to observe a number of naked men standing tall, while an equal number of naked men kneeled in front of them, slashing away with safety razors at their pubic parts.

Detroit, Lawson and myself, so reluctant to part with something we had waited for so long to grow, held out for the deadline.

This was to be a fateful decision, since about two hours later the base doctor rushed in and asked: "What the hell is going on here?"

Seems one recruit had been accidentally slashed in the orgy and showed up at the dispensary almost castrated.

The doctor dispensed crab ointments and chewed out Maluski.

Maluski never forgave the three of us for remaining unshorn, and we ran up a camp record for shit details that hasn't been exceeded to this day.

But I always try to look at the positive side. How many other recruits derived the benefits of learning how to scrub a whole barracks latrine with a toothbrush?

Take Me, I'm Yours

You might get the wrong impression from these first chapters. This is not an attempt to write a titillating tale, but only to tell in the raw "the way it was" in those earliest training days.

When you surrendered yourself to the military, you surrendered sovereignty over your own body. They tell you when it should be dressed, what it should wear, and when it should be naked. And in those early days, there was a lot of naked.

To call us "privates" was absurd. If we were anything, we were "publics." Anyone who had a shred of modesty had better lose it quickly.

The most public of all was "short arm inspection." Why they didn't call it "short leg" escapes me.

It is the military's periodic check for signs of drainage from venereal diseases.

A medic sits on a stool while the line of nakeds advance upon him to milk the member.

He sees all shapes, sizes and styles, while ignoring the same old nervous jokes.

"This makes me think of my favorite cow!"

Circumcision being much less common in those days: "I know it's in there somewhere, Doc!"

Length: "Sorry, Doc, but it takes two hands to do this!"

The medics had their comebacks: "That thing ever bruise your knees?"

Or, "Hank, bring the magnifying glass!"

Putting me through such an exam was a waste of time.

When it came to the premarital sex norms of fifty years ago, I was a world-class conformist.

Who wouldn't be, after viewing the Armed Force's answer to the "Joy of Sex?"

Every home should have a video copy of the Army's short movie on the slimy ravages of venereal disease upon man's favorite tool: "She may look clean, but...."

If someone takes poison, just show it to him. You will get it all back fast.

CULTURAL IMPERATIVES

The cultural norms in our camp were given a kick in the balls when it developed that I, an apartment dwelling city boy, was one of the two best rifle shots in the battalion. The other was a boy from the hills of Kentucky, who eschewed rifle sights and aimed down the side of the barrel. "Kentucky windage" it was called.

I was a city boy trespassing upon the domain reserved for the Hatfields and McCoys. This was their "Cultural Imperative." In other words, "Stay off of our pruppety!"

I was not about to! The tensions and prejudices were rising.

Then, the Lord intervened on their behalf and mine.

So long as we were going single shot on the range, the Kentucky boy and I were neck and neck, but I soon discovered that in a right-handed world a left-handed shooter doesn't have a chance with a right-hand loading Garand M-1 on the fast fire and reload range. Just try to match another guy's accuracy in a 15 second shoot-off when you are trying to reload your right-handed gun with your left hand.

Finally, any city guy who whips out a book during rest breaks has got to be looked upon as an eccentric no matter where he hails from, so I was impelled to establish my credentials as a "regular guy."

After falling on my face in the rapid reload shoot-off, I trotted out my four years of experience beering and bowling at the 22nd Street pool rooms with the Polish boys in Chicago and joined the other recruits on their carousing about the nearby towns.

Once I had establish my credentials as a leisure time screw-off, they certified me as an "OK guy" and I was free to withdraw to my eccentricities.

IMAGE

Hand in hand with cultural variations runs the phenomenon of "Image."

The closer the candidate for acting non-commissioned officer matches the movie star W.A.S.P image, the more likely he is to be selected.

I didn't see too many of this type leading in combat, but on the parade grounds they were ubiquitous.

I guessed instantly that the acting First Sergeant would be that tall, athletic suburban model who dived so gracefully at the pool. All others will be matched against him.

You could be certain that no ethnic types would be chosen until that pool of talent was exhausted, and in our case, it was inexhaustible.

Each of us was interviewed. For example, there was me:

"Any military training?"

"R.O.T.C. Four years. High school."

"Highest rank reached?"

"First Lieutenant."

"Drill field experience?"

"Platoons, companies, and Drum Major of the military marching band that won the award at the annual Chicago high school R.O.T.C. parade down Michigan Avenue in 1943."

Great credentials, right?

Wrong!

Suburban boy got company Acting First Sergeant.

Workmacher got platoon Acting Sergeant.

Jenkins, Minnesota, and Lawson were made squad Acting Corporals, and Riccarili and I were the head and tail ends of Jenkins's squad.

That was the nature of the barracks and parade field army in those days. You will see later that, in combat, all that shit goes out of the window and effectiveness is the criteria. But as soon as combat ends, the parade-field heroes re-emerge.

THANKS FOR THE MEMORIES

It is impossible to remember all of the eleven weeks of basic training of sixty-four years ago, but certain memories linger on.

What endure the most are those things that did the greatest violence to my established concepts of civility.

One day, early on, one of fellows asked me, "Do you know where Jenkins and the others go every night after chow?" No, I didn't.

"They go down to the back fence to have sex with their wives and girl friends."

I did a double take!

It's true that a few of the guys had their women come down to live in the town, and had weekends to spend with them, but "How do they get out without passes?"

"They don't! They 'do it' through the fences."

Just visualizing this activity through the wiring of a cyclone fence still gives me a pain in the wrong place.

I really didn't believe him, so I up front asked my acting corporal, Jenkins, if he really did that with his wife.

"Sure! What do you think she's here for?"

A bash in the brain!

Minnesota delighted in telling us stories of sex with his wife. He particularly relished telling of sitting her on some flat surface such as a table, a sink or such, and bam! He would punch his palm.

His "piece de resistance" was the time they forgot they had left the burner on when he sat her on the electric stove and, "Now, she's got my brand on her ass for life," he cackled.

This denigration of wives boggled me. In all the ethnic environments in which I had ever dwelt, one would talk like this about the "easy marks," but not one's own wife. These were supposed to be the Madonnas!

On second thought, why should I even reflect on these cultural variations?

I imagine by this time Jenkins has already sat across the table from his son over a couple of beers and said: "I knew this guy in basic training. Strange guy! He would rather go to a movie or get books from the library than beer with us at the PX.

"And, he got the strangest look on his face when I told him I screwed your mother through a cyclone fence!"

Minnesota was a strange bird. At five-foot-five, with the map of Sweden on his face, he built up this story of owning a big business in St. Paul and turning down a commission to serve in the ranks.

Because I was young and naive, I did not doubt him, especially since he was a very generous buyer of rounds of beers for the boys in the PX. I soon had reason to doubt.

Jenkins, from some southern state, was not too bright, but a really generous guy. Despite his limited financial resources, he nevertheless, invited our squad to spend a weekend pass at the shack he had rented for his wife and two children at an extortionist rate from a local "patriot."

The only condition he made, only half jokingly, is that we stay out of his wife's pants. I didn't find that too hard to agree to.

On Sunday afternoon, while I was swinging in the hammock in the back yard, Jenkins, came out with a blanched look and said: "Someone has stolen our allotment money off the dresser!"

Now to most readers, the loss of fifty dollars, even in 1944 may not seem devastating, but to Jenkins and his family, refugees from a pocket of poverty, it was catastrophic. They lived financially from month to month. They were truly distraught.

I, because I had been watching the baby and snoozing in the hammock all afternoon in full view of Jenkins and his wife, was the only one beyond suspicion. Minnesota, showing great sympathy, led the charge around the house looking for the lost cash.

Back in camp the next day, it became a "cause célèbre" and each of the visitors, other than myself, were called into the Captain's office for interrogation.

Minnesota was so concerned that he started a collection for the Jenkins family with a ten dollar bill, and soon we had all pitched in more than the fifty dollars they had lost.

To celebrate, Minnesota took us all over to the PX for a treat round of beer . When he threw the money down on the table, Jenkins eyes froze on it. He grabbed Minnesota's wrist. "You son-of-a-bitch! That's my money!"

Minnesota pulled his arm away: "What the hell you talking about?"

"That five dollar bill!" He picked it up and smelled it. "That's where my kid pooped on the dresser, and that smear is where I wiped it off!"

The next day, Minnesota was transferred to another company.

CARPETBAGGERS

The citizens of the local town, numbering hundreds, were overwhelmed by the tens of thousands of trainees that were routed through the camp.

Despite this, they were gracious, and operated some nice canteen centers for the troops.

It was the carpetbaggers that gave the town a bad name, the vermin that funnel into any place where young, naive military are concentrated in order to pluck the innocent.

Mine was a minor incident which only demonstrates the larger problem.

I bought a cigarette lighter for five dollars in one of the clip joints they operated. That was a large sum for a trainee in those days.

After I filled it with fluid, I couldn't get it to operate. One of the other guys looked at it and said: "This thing is junk! It was broken and they soldered it back in reverse."

I went back the next Saturday evening and the owner wouldn't even talk to me. I was getting hot. He went to the door and called the Military Policeman on the street who removed me.

I was trying to explain to the MP what had happened and he said: "I know! I know! This happens all the time with those bastards, but there is nothing we can do about it. That is free enterprise and we are not permitted to intervene in civilian affairs."

I was standing there utterly frustrated when the Farm Boy Machos walked up.

I told them my story. Workmacher, the main stud, took the lighter from me and said, "Come on, boys!" And we walked into the store.

"I understand you sold my brother, here, a bum lighter."

All activity in the store stopped. You have to know that these people were looking at the equivalent of five Belgium draft horses.

"Harry, call the MPs!"

Hank caught Harry's arm as he passed.

Customers were beginning to move to the far corners of the store.

"Joseph," said Workmacher, "Where are the MPs?"

Joseph looked out of the door. "About a block down!"

Workmacher took the edge of one glass cabinet and tilted it back and forth: "How much do you reckon we can trash in this place before they get here? You think we can do more than five dollars worth?"

The owner had his hand to his mouth, totally blanched: "You questioning my honesty?"

"No question about that!"

"OK, OK, here's the five bucks."

It was wonderful to see justice prevail. The problem was that there were hundreds of thousands of boys serving their country that didn't have the Farm Boy Machos to enforce it for them.

SMILES

It wasn't only outside forces that preyed upon servicemen. There was the enemy within. Ask any veteran who went through a replacement training camp what the worst barracks problem was, and he will answer without hesitation, "Theft!"

Just dare to leave your footlocker open and unattended, and you have brought your own problem down upon yourself.

Many times, one rushes out to formation without socks because one has turned his back while dressing. I have even gone out without underwear.

I was a high school track man so I thought I could make it to the latrine to retrieve my razor and be back in time, but the thief's hand moves faster that the victim's foot.

With the exception of Texas, who was lying on the next bunk bed contemplating the mattress above, all the rest of the company was congregated at the latrine end. When I shot back out of the latrine and down the aisle, nothing had changed.

When I got back to my open foot locker, Texas got up and walked out of the Barracks.

It wasn't until I got to the "put on the watch" part of my dressing that I realized it was missing. That watch was something I had wanted for a long time. It was a graduation present, a gold Gruen curved dress watch.

I tore the foot locker apart, and then I realized only Texas could have taken it. I sat down and waited for him to come back.

A half hour later, he did. "Where's my watch, Texas?"

He smiled. Texas always smiled. Everyone loved Texas because he always smiled. He smiled himself through basic. He smiled his way through Germany until he got hit in the head by a mortar shell.

Because he always smiled everybody believed him. Because he smiled everybody loved him. He never defended himself. He never needed to. He always smiled.

I wish I had learned how to smile like that. I could have supported myself in luxury.

THE PERCUSSION SECTION

I came to regret my shooting accuracy when we went onto the 57 mm anti-tank gun range during the last two weeks of our training. Prior to this, we had "dry run" practice by tracking little toy tanks at a distance of about twenty feet, and firing 22 caliber rifles mounted on the barrels of the larger weapons.

In those days, it took twelve men and a truck to move and operate each of these ordinance, and we finally did set up on a real range, firing real shells at real scrap tanks being pulled by chains about 100 yards away.

Chance had it that I was the first gunner on our line, with forty other positions flanking us. A judge stood behind each unit.

The order was given to: "Fire!" And we all pulled the trigger levers simultaneously.

What follows still shudders in my memory. Instead of a smattering of little 22 caliber rifle pops, there was this combined full-throated roar of all forty-one full-grown 57 mm guns.

I still knelt, totally frozen, my ears playing variations on "Jingle Bells", contemplating the gravel now embedded in my thighs and knees.

The officers were off chasing and trying to stop the other eleven trainees from each gun.

I determined: "I will not qualify as a 57 mm anti-tank gunner!"

I stuffed my ears each day with half a package of cotton and wrapped towels around my thighs under my fatigues. We rotated as gunners each day until we had all taken ten shots.

I had to be careful each time I was up at bat that the umpire behind me did not detect my attempts to bunt fouls.

I shot at the ground in front of the tank. The shell bounced up and hit.

"Hit!" said the umpire.

I tried shooting over the tank. It dropped into the turret.

"Hit!" said the umpire.

I shot in front, just as the chain lurched. You guessed it.

"Hit!" said the umpire.

In short, I hit 6 out of 10 shots, enough to qualify me for the award as the best anti-tank gunner in the battalion.

As I accepted the award with my ears still ringing, I realized that my symphonic career was coming to a premature end.

HELL ON EARTH

My most pervasive memory of Basic Training is the heat.

If any movie company wants to do location shot of Hades it would be our Texas camp that summer.

The heat struck the camp the afternoon we got off the buses.

The sun was so severe that our regular army company commander, after five successive bouts of skin peeling, was hospitalized, never to return.

Lesson One was: The bigger you were the quicker you fell. It was the skinny city boys, like Riccarili and me, who were helping the Farm Boy Machos back to the barracks.

Lesson Two: If you are going to fall, watch out for the cactus. It was a toss up as to which was worse, the prickly heat or the cactus.

I voted for the cactus, because the prickly heat was gone before all the cactus needles made it back out of my behind.

If you haven't had prickly heat, be advised that every muscle movement is agony, represented by a pincushion full of needle pricks with every gesture. It got so bad that I even hated to use the latrine.

I thought then that nothing worse could happen to us, weather-wise.

I was wrong!

The first day we moved out of the barracks into the field for maneuvers it started to rain, non-stop. We were shooting water guns as well as bullets. Our tents floated away-- while we were trying to sleep in them. Our food was "Add water and serve".

I have said this seriously before, and I will repeat it now:

Other than the possibility of becoming a casualty, combat living conditions were a vacation compared to Basic Training.

On the last day of our two week bivouac, the rains suddenly stopped. Of course! We were done!

Faces and uniforms caked with mud, we began our march back to the trucks.

We came upon one of those clear, narrow streams that cut their way neatly through the limestone of central Texas.

The Sergeant looked at it longingly for a moment and then said: "Left face! Forward march!" And we marched straight into the stream, uniform, packs, rifles and all.

A river of mud began to flow downstream, followed by socks, pants, jackets, shirts, underpants, and undershirts.

There, in waist deep water, stood a company of naked men, dipping the mud off of their weapons and falling back into the water in ecstasy.

We had returned from Hell! The river Jordan! We were baptized!

The Promised Land!

We were full fledged soldiers!

SNAFU

The most common term used in the U.S. Army was SNAFU , an acronym for "Situation normal, all fouled up!"

Seven in our company, including me, were trained for a job we would never do. We were too young to go overseas to be the replacements we spent eleven weeks training for.

Instead of tickets for overseas, we were given marching orders to an Army division still in the United States.

First, however, a short furlough home to prove to my mother that I was healthy enough for the Army. I had gone from 129 pounds to a muscle-packed 145.

"My God! He's healthy! What did they feed you? You never ate at home!"

I didn't have the heart to tell her, it was chicken that hadn't had all the nourishment boiled out of it, meat that hadn't been cooked to nutritional extinction, no garlic salt to make me throw up the little nourishment I had ingested, nor that until the Army, I hadn't know how good food could taste.

I was the neighborhood knockout! What muscle I had was packed down and wrapped in a form-fitting Eisenhower jacket. The local matchmakers were mentally lining up mates for me.

THE BOYS IN THE FIRST BATTALION

When I arrived at the division camp in the Southland, I was surprised to discover that I had been assigned to the first battalion medical aid station of the first regiment. The rational was that I would be trained within the unit itself.

The aid station was a mixed bag drawn from all over the country. The entire division had been in training for a year-and-a-half as a reserve unit to be called to either of the theatres of war when needed.

The only other newcomers in our unit were eight former college boys who had enlisted to be trained as fighter pilots. Six months before, when the need for more pilots evaporated, they were, of course, dropped into infantry units as replacements.   So as was common in the Army in those days, the brightest boys were subordinated to grunt non-coms.

They were very bitter!

The two I remember most were Hoffman and Lerner.

Hoffman was a full-fledged scion of the American aristocracy, who would have most certainly become an officer if he had not betrayed himself into believing the army's commitment to train him to be a "fly boy". He blamed this only on a Democratic Administration. Of course, a Republican Administration would have never betrayed him so! Sure!

He was a blond, full-bodied, cigar-smoking, All Ivy League football lineman as well as an honor student. Assured, confident and aloof, he sort of left me in a state of awe.

Lerner, out of a well-to-do New York Jewish family, was dark, handsome, athletically built, a Columbia University graduate, and utterly indifferent to anything that went on in our unit. He would neither bathe nor shave regularly, nor ever fall out for any of our Battalion training or formations. All he would do during the day, other than go to meals, was sit on his bunk, playing out bridge hands and chess games.

The unit leaders, embarrassed by the fate of these disenfranchised aristocrats left him strictly alone.

Other early impressions:

First Sergeant Wagner was a skinny, very hyper, four year veteran who had no real interest in our outfit other that seeing to it that we did not screw up weekend passes. He was passionately in love with his wife, a native of the town, whom he looked upon as a Madonna, that other non-coms from first-hand knowledge knew to be a whore. Woe unto anyone whose feasance, misfeasance, or malfeasance aborted his weekend passions with his wife!

Sergeant Adams, second highest ranking non-com, was really the highest ranking medical technician. He looked, acted, and spoke very much like a young Harry Truman, complete to the wire rimmed eyeglasses. In civilian life, he was an ordained Methodist minister from a small town in northern Wisconsin who, to his credit, chose the infinitely more dangerous job of combat medic over a certain commissioned officer's job as a Chaplain. The unit for the most part hated him for his chicken-shit and righteous insistence upon meticulous observances of the rules and regulations.

Sergeant Bruce was a company aid man. His father owned the biggest auto agency in a small town in Ohio, setting up their status as the dominant financial patrons of the local Presbyterian Church. Bruce was the quintessential fraternity boy. He was dedicated to becoming a war hero, and coming home to local honor, glory and prominence. He had no doubts regarding his destiny and he aggressively projected that image in every one of our exercises. He was just dying to get into combat. I had the contrary feeling, that if he got into combat, he would die. I proved to be right.

Then there was Sergeant Shapiro, who headed up the dispensary. He was a liberal Jewish pre-med from the Bronx, whom I sensed was a very smart and a subtle operator who would deal with the devil if need be to assure a safe return to his medical career. He would quietly do good for anyone so long it did not stir up "the powers-that-be."

He had inestimable value to me as a source of information regarding the dynamics of the group.

His assistant was Corporal Walsh, New York City, with an overlay of conviviality that masked his contempt toward anyone who was not Catholic or Republican. He took pains to make sure that everyone knew his circumcision was the result of a teen age indiscretion, not a conversion.

MY SQUAD

With no medical training, another newcomer, Lawson, and I were assigned to a litter bearer squad under Corporal "Missouri," who looked upon himself as a continuing country-boy comedy act.

The other member was Pfc. Watters a quiet, strong fellow from Kansas without any pretensions to independent thought, who followed Missouri like a shadow.

Lawson, like me, was a "too-young-for-combat" reject. He was an eastern prep school product whose father was the vice- president of a large corporation. We were an unlikely pair, having in common only an interest in Northwestern University, This bonding undoubtedly saved our sanity in the early days of combat.

No sooner had our belated training started when the Division was finally alerted for overseas duty. The Allies were advancing in both theaters of operation, so we had no idea which direction we would be going, South Pacific or Europe.

Still being 18, Lawson and I could have petitioned out of going, but we decided to let fate play its hand. The hope that we would get some medical training before combat never materialized, and this was to plague us in all the days to come.

We had all had seen returning veterans, so no one wanted to go to the Pacific Theater. We were a very nervous bunch as our train moved North. Then, at 3:00 AM on the third morning someone raced through the cars yelling, "We turned East! We're going to Europe!" A cheer rang through the length of the train.

THE CLASS STRUGGLE

A bemused band of Cleveland commuters hustled to their trains that early November morning in 1944.

They needed to skirt the ranks of about a hundred soldiers in neat formation on the concrete apron bordering the troop train.

In the Army, morning calisthenics are as religiously observed as Catholic masses, so long as any flat piece of land could be found for the health worshipers.

In front, leading the services, was a young, trim, athletic second lieutenant, so fresh and agile that his very steps had a spring to them.

Some commuters stopped to watch as the services proceeded methodically through the ritual, culminating in the ultimate recessional: "Side Straddle Hop, Commence!"

This, if you are not familiar with the exercise, is called "Jumping Jacks" and goes from the position of attention to a hop in the air coming down with legs spread while simultaneously doing a "high five" with one's own finger tips. Generally, the supplicants continue until they drop out voluntarily at their own limit, while the others continue to theirs.

This particular lieutenant was a bouncy, proud bundle of agility, energy and endurance.

I dropped out at the count of one hundred grasping my aching lungs, and moved to join the others at the sidelines.

The lieutenant looked fresh as a daisy, as if he had just begun the morning exercises. More and more soldiers were dropping out and moving to the sidelines, until, at the count of two hundred, there were only about ten still hopping.

The lieutenant was laid back:

"You...can...drop...out...any...time!" beautifully timed to each of his still springy hops.

The survivors were now up to three hundred hops. Only three enlisted men remained. The lieutenant was still "hoppity" fresh and still gracious:

"You...can...drop...out...any...time!"

At the count of five hundred, all were at the sidelines, except for one country boy toward the back. Civilians, other military units, and officers were gathering to watch.

"Yawl can drop out anytime 'tenant!" said the survivor.

The lieutenant's jaw hardened and he picked up the pace. Soon, his breathe was failing him, so another officer stepped forward and picked up the count. Everyone, hundreds, were moving in closer to observe the drama unfolding before them.

The lieutenant's face got redder and then began to blanch. There was now more to this than just a morning exercise. This was a class struggle and he was carrying with his hops the whole burden of "fitness to lead" for the ruling class. The officers were fading over in his direction while the enlisted men moved toward the soldier.

Then, a single voice: "C'mon Clem! Show him what we've got!" Clem nodded and picked up the pace. A roar of shouts went up urging Clem on.

The officers, meanwhile, were putting on some cheering for the lieutenant.

I lost count. At a thousand something, the lieutenant stopped dead at attention, eyes rolled up and his trim young body fell backward onto the platform with a sickening thud.

The officers raced over and bent over him. Then, one straightened up and yelled: "MEDIC!"

The grateful underclass were mobbing Clem, who was still hopping.

Then, he stopped, breathing a little heavily, and wiped his brow with an undershirt someone donated.

Everyone was hitting him on the back and smiling.

"Shucks!" he said: "Twarnt nothin'! Just lucky I put my jockstrap on this morning!"

From such random incidents are revolutions born!

Part II
Over There

OVER THERE!

We got the usual U.S.O. treatment in New York before we boarded a coastal excursion ship never intended for trans-oceanic travel. But it was a luxury liner compared to the bobbing victory ships in our convoy. There aren't as many green faces on Mars as there were on the emaciated victory ship troops that disembarked in Marseilles.

Except for me, our boys were in pretty good shape by then. Ironically, I am generally one of the last to succumb to things, so Pvt. Peters, from South Carolina and I spent most of the early part of the trip, mopping up, feeding, helping all of the others to the johns.

Then, when all were recovered and playing cards, shooting dice and doing other military necessities, I went under.

I lay in my bunk dehydrating for days, totally ignored, even by Peters who would rather have died than shown weakness.

With nothing else to do for ten or more days, gambling aboard troop ships became the stuff of legends. Every GI has heard stories of tens of thousands of dollars being won by skilled players on these voyages, and we had one who damn well matched that by the time we debarked in Europe. He was said later to have commented, when hearing of the combat death of one of his card-playing buddies, "That son-of-bitch can't pull that! He still owes me five thousand dollars!"

Meanwhile, the hated Regimental First Sergeant, Mahar, had disappeared after boarding. Only a few of the officers knew where he was hiding and they wouldn't tell.

All through the voyage, the corridors of the ship echoed with the voices of his victims singing a parody of the old song, "Abdul A Bul Bul Amir":

"A splash in the water, one dark moonlight night,

"Sent ripples that went wide and far,

"Was caused by a sack fitting close the back,

"Of Abdul A Bul Bul MAHAR!"

No wonder he didn't show up!

He finally reappeared when we landed in Marseilles.

We disembarked and loaded onto some trucks on the quay. While we were waiting, looking at the masts of sunken and scuttled ships poking out of the harbor waters, a rifleman walked by: "This has got to be the smartest danged country in the world. Everyone of them little kids can speak French!"

MT. ZION

The temporary city that our Division created that early winter's day on that plateau overlooking Marseilles is a wonder to me to this day. In a matter of twenty-four hours, a flat piece of barren, inhospitable land was turned into a city of streets, lights, kitchens and services with American inventiveness.

The area had been denuded of virtually every stick of wood by the previous divisions that had occupied it, so we spent most of our days scouring for every sliver or leaf we could find for our fires, while we gradually accumulated that characteristic patina of dirt and grime that so distinguishes the "dog-face" rifleman from his more sheltered fellow warriors.

A religious revival occurred spontaneously. Just about everyone attended makeshift chapels or temples of some denomination or another. How quickly intimations of mortality revives our interest in the Deity!

Since I had no religious commitment at all, I made the rounds of all of them. If nothing else, they were momentarily damn warm interiors on that windswept desert.

I remember walking back from Jewish services with Rothstein, a boy from Los Angeles who was a litter bearer in the second battalion aid station. He bore a pessimism that even my mother would have envied.

The setting was really primitive. The young Chaplain had commandeered a tool shed and had gone into town for some wine. The altar was a barrel with little white candles for light.

Pretty soon the shed was packed with unshaven, unkempt, smelly soldiers. The more that packed in, of course, the warmer it got. Thank God for this burst of piety!

Maybe some were drinking the wine for sacramental purposes, but, I was drinking it for warmth.

What kept the services short was that our feet began to freeze.

Rothstein was certain he was going to die. To me, who bore the belief that he would be only an observer at this event, that possibility struck me as unthinkable.

I argued with him all the way back to the tents, but to no avail.

Every time I ran into him later I would kid, "Well, Rothstein! Still alive?" He didn't think that was funny.

You can imagine what kind of an ass I felt like when his team was the first to die in combat. The Germans infiltrated through the lines one night and blasted all four in their foxhole.

Those who revealed to me that they expected to die ran a close second to the "wannabe heroes" in the casualty count. I won't guess whether there was some metaphysical relationship.

Later, when things got desperate in the foxholes, I did a lot of unaccustomed praying and bargaining with God. After that, I felt that it would be unseemly for me to continue to be an atheist anymore, so I promoted God to Agnostic. I hadn't made it up to theist yet, but I was still young.

Our New Leaders

On our last night in the encampment, Sgt. Adams was made Acting First Sergeant of our aid station. Sgt. Wagner was no longer functioning. The further geographically we were removed from his wife, the deeper his depression became. By the time we encamped, he was being led around to food and the latrine, and being dressed and undressed by the other non-coms. He was a virtual Zombie. His condition was an embarrassment to a medical detachment, so it was decided to hold on to him and hope for rapid recovery.

That night a man appeared who would set in motion the machinery of change in my self-image, our new doctor, Captain Wilson. In a surprise to us, he was replacing our previous doctor who was being transferred to a field hospital.

He was affable, appeared democratic and openly courted everyone's favor. I was impressed.

Shapiro whispered to me: "He is dangerous!"

He was right.

Captain Wilson was a doctor who had been a partner in a very successful medical group in a Midwestern city.

Beside being an excellent doctor, he was immensely money, status and power conscious and brooked not one iota of insubordination from anyone. No hospital nurse. No medical assistant. No medical associate. No one. He needed to be completely in charge of his own turf while courting the power at the next level up. It was not a pleasant combination for those whom the Army imprisoned under his control.

In no time, he had manipulated Major Hopkins, our Battalion Commander and surgeon, who specialized in "dim wit," and that court of appeals was closed to us also.

I was to see this again and again in later years: Men and women brilliant in the humanities, science, arts and management who, at the personal level, were inhumane, indifferent and callus.

Poor Lieutenant Herman, our medical administrative officer, was a humane, if quixotic, former investment banker who saw war as a romanticized Hemingway adventure. Like Inspector Clouseau he never came to understand the mischief that would be practiced upon him by his superior.

DOGFIGHT

The one and only movie-type dogfight we ever saw was while we were waiting in trucks to move out of Marseilles.

There were eighteen planes wheeling and shooting about the sky.

Lt. Herman was scouring the expanse with his enormous field glasses and counted sixteen American and two German planes.

They wheeled and shot and wheeled and shot, until finally one came smoking straight down into the field adjoining us. We were cheering like crazy while some ran out to see the smoking wreckage.

Lt. Herman kept scouring the sky. There were two planes now streaking East toward Germany.

Herman turned his head to us. "My God! We shot down our own plane!"

THE MOMENT OF TRUTH

Our battalion was moved for further training to an abandoned two-story modern factory about 50 kilometers north of Marseilles.

After we set up on the second floor, I took a walk to a nearby village.

When I returned, Lawson was standing at the door looking very pale: "Hoffman is dead!"

I was unable to comprehend.

"I'm telling you Hoffman is dead! He was lying on the floor reading, when a rifleman downstairs cleared his rifle and shot him in the back."

The power of military drilling! Empty your magazine, then point the muzzle up and pull the trigger, in case you forgot the bullet in the chamber. BUT NOT IN A BUILDING, YOU STUPID!

Our first casualty!

I staggered off mindlessly, walking faster and faster, actually sobbing!

Hoffman! If there was ever anyone who had everything! Who had it made! Who had everything to live for!

To what advantage luxury? To what advantage prep schools? To what advantage Ivy League and football field glory? To what advantage all of the training in social graces and education? Death is the great social leveler. You can't take it with you!

Now, I was internalizing the truth. This isn't a movie. I am not just a passive observer. This is for real!

We are all facing our moments of truth.

THE TRANS-FRANCE CHOO CHOO

Our pre-combat training never commenced.

It was December, and we were needed to fill a gap left in the 7th Army lines by the Battle of the Bulge.

We were loaded onto 40-and-8 freight cars, leftovers of World War I, for our trip north.

If you don't know what these are, in winter they are the most miserable transportation conceived by man. They are wooden freight cars with gaps in the boards of the sides and the floor, intended for 40 men or 8 horses. The French deemed these not good enough for horses.

For three days and nights, we huddled under blankets and equipment hoping to keep our frozen bones from cracking in the cold winds that whistled through the apertures.

Cut down to such a primitive survival mode, values change.

Quarrels commenced over who had the warmer corner or who had the extra blanket. Had you exceeded your allotted time at the aid station stove?

Fighting erupts over a fruit bar in a K-ration box. A candy bar in a 40-and-8 is worth a chateaubriand at Maxim's in Paris. Nerves are raw and friendships are tested.

We were all miserable.

Finally, we debarked at a town bordering the Saar River where Lt. Herman had liberated a functioning chateau.

I remember a scene in a movie, where a soldier walks into the mirrored room of such a chateau and, seeing a disheveled, uniformed stranger fires his gun and shatters the mirror.

If I had carried a gun, I would have done the same thing.

I looked horrible! Hair shortened into crew cut ruts by a bandage scissors, face filthy and bearded, horrible scrawny blonde moustache, mud-caked battle jacket, smelling like the horses in a 40-and-8.... Is this the sexy soldier who left Chicago last September?

RESURRECTION

In any war, in any country, American soldiers find that there are young enterprisers who attach themselves to the units and, for a price, can become agents to arrange for any needs, be it washing, cooking, prostitutes, whatever.

Such a lad was Wilhelm, a bright Alsatian boy of 11, who spoke a pretty good brand of English.

Pretty soon, I had clean clothes, fresh croissants, and had been scrubbed clean by some of the French "Mamas" who resided in the buildings across from the chateau.

Shortly, we had covered the broken panes, started the tile oven, set up the aid station, and had made ourselves quite comfortable.

I was developing a genuine respect for what the country boys were able to do to make life livable.

The South Carolinian, Peters, had gotten hold of some eggs and other ingredients and, adding these to our K and C rations, cooked up a pretty good meal on our aid station stove.

Unfortunately, when basic needs are met, socialization recommences and political, religious and social differences interface again.

Generally, advocates lined up in two camps: Republican country folks versus urban Democrats. Suburbanism wasn't even that important, yet.

We had this Dutch-style tile oven that stood about six feet tall. The radiation from the heated tiles did a pretty good job of heating the main room.

Problem was, having no coal or kindling, we had to ignite some local coke by drenching it with gasoline from our jeep.

We were standing in confrontational lines in the center of the room while Detroit was igniting the coke.

He straightened up to listen. By the time he bent over again to ignite his Zippo lighter, the gasoline fumes had drifted into the room.

There was an enormous "pouff" and a sheet of flames passed between the two factions. The oven opened gaps in the tiles and soot was drifting through the room and covering everything like black snow in a crystal winter scene.

Detroit lost his eyebrows and the forelocks of his hair.

Covered with soot, Shapiro raised his forefinger: "God has spoken!"

We never discussed politics or religion again.

THE MIRACLE CURE

We were in business!

Our first casualty arrived that night.

A jeep from a company that had been on the line for some time brought in a man wounded in the right foot.

He would get no purple heart for this, as he had "accidentally" inflicted it upon himself while riding.

I put quotes around the word accidentally, because we were told that as Christmas approached and the miserable drifting snows were deepening, there had been a rising incidence of such "accidents".

There was no dreaming of a White Christmas here! Bing Crosby would have been shot dead in his tracks.

Shortly, thereafter, I saw my first "psycho" case. The rifleman was led in bent over like an ape with his arms dangling. I was to see this, later, again and again, during heavy fighting and bombardments.

He was placed on the table, his eyes blankly staring at the ceiling. The Captain tried any number of things to bring him back, including ammonia capsules, but, finally, Shapiro began writing up the tag that would be his ticket to a rear area psycho ward.

"May I try, Captain?" asked Corporal Walsh. Wilson waved him to the table.

Walsh unbuckled the man's pants and pulled them and his shorts down to his knees. I wondered what this part of his anatomy had to do with his brain.

Then, he grasped masses of pubic hair between his knuckles and pulled his hands up sharply. There was a shriek and the man jumped up, tripping on his trousers as he was swinging at Walsh.

Corporal Walsh, product of the streets of New York, in the face of the failure of modern medicine and psychiatry, had administered a miraculous native home cure for this mystifying mental disorder!

Later, when I observed genuine cases of the malady that this rifleman was faking, something termed "battle rattles", I was genuinely shocked at the physical manifestations.

Some of the victims would be led in by a buddy who would be holding him by the hand while he looked like a stooped-over ape or orangutan and would actually be exhibiting only basic simian conduct.

One of the most common catalysts was being stuck overnight in a foxhole with a dead buddy, but any sort of shock could set this off.

Whatever the reason, I hope that no reader will ever need experience viewing such a Darwinian regression in a human being.

THE UNTRAINED MEDIC

The next morning, I had my first run-in with Captain Wilson.

He hardly ever noticed litter bearers, who were too far down the local social scale, but spotting me, he asked that I start a fire in his bedroom stove.

I had never started an open fire in my life! I was a lifelong apartment dweller from Chicago.

Nevertheless, I struggled for over an hour. Crumpled up paper and charred kindling were all over the floor when Wilson came in, went into a rage, threw me out, and got someone else to do it.

As luck would have it, before I got out of the aid station, a litter team brought in a soldier who had stepped on a land mine. His mangled leg was bleeding badly.

Wilson pushed me aside as he raced to the table. He looked and then reached back to me: "Get me a hemostat!"

I looked at the instrument table helplessly. I had no training. I did not even know what a hemostat was.

Wilson looked around over his outstretched hand: "Don't you know anything? Get the hell out of here! Shapiro, come here!"

I slunk out of the back door.

Shapiro, the humanist, came in the great room later, where I was sitting on my bed slumped over and looking at the floor.

He put his arm around me.

"I'll explain to the Captain. I've had no training," I said.

"Stay away from him! He won't listen or understand. Nobody else means anything to him."

"How the hell do you get along with him?"

"By being his lackey! Your problem is that you are proud.

"You aren't willing to stick your head halfway up his ass in order to survive, like I am. And, if I do survive and I do get out, I will thumb my nose at the bastard, and say: 'Fuck you, Captain Doctor!'"

"I can't do that!"

"I know you can't! So stay out of his sight, or he'll send you out as a company aid man for sure!"

I need to explain the significance of that comment.

In the narrow little world of combat, mere yards can determine whether you live or die.

The Army's highest combat casualty rates are not the line infantrymen, but the company and platoon medics who must move to the wounded while riflemen cling to cover.

Litter bearers, who are able to control their own movements, somewhat, have a sharply lower casualty rate than the platoon aidmen.

Aid stations, while they may be only thousands of yards back, unless they are hit by a shell, are not generally targets in combat and rarely suffer severe casualties.

So, being sent out as a company aid man from a battalion aid station is like being sent to your death.

It had been sort of an unwritten code of vest pocket justice to replace company aidmen casualties from the division replacement pool, and the same for litter bearers and aid station personnel. It was very demoralizing for the latter to be threatened with being sent out to the foxholes. But that was the Captain's ultimate revenge upon those who did not knuckle under to his domination.

Meanwhile, at every opportunity, Shapiro would gather the untrained litter bearers for a crash course in first aid techniques that the others had spent years in Army schools acquiring.

10,000 BOMBERS

A new phenomena commenced.

One morning, we heard an overhead droning, and we rushed outside to look.

It was the beginning of what came to be know as the "ten thousand plane raids."

Tightly-packed bombers were slowly droning from west to east overhead. The noise was awesome.

This lasted from about ten in the morning to noon.

After spending two hours making mashed potatoes of Germany, the return flights east to west passed overhead at about two o'clock until about four o'clock in the afternoon.

The truth was that the defensive Luftwaffe was past history and Germany was helpless to defend itself from the air.

The truth was also that we heavily outnumbered the troops the Germans were committing to the Western Front because they were trying to hold off the Russians in the East.

In any given engagement, however, troop quantities were more even, but we had the advantage of being able to soften them up with some awesome artillery and air support before we moved.

While in the East the Russians were taking horrendous casualties, we were, with the exception of General Patton, doing the best we could to reduce the number of our own losses.

Actually, it was a test at times for our own Seventh army, under a careful General Patch, to keep contact with the southern perimeter of an aggressive General Patton.

MERRY CHRISTMAS!

Christmas Eve, 1944, on the German-American front was a strange evening, similarly reported in many other books.

Up and down the lines the air was still, the night was cold, the moon was out and the guns were silent.

Each listened to the other singing Christmas carols across "no-man's land."

Company B had sent over a bottle of schnapps that a patrol had liberated across the river. We saved it for this evening.

The Captain was unusually affable as he uncorked the clear liquid and passed down the line of celebrants, filling the paper cups we had filched from the dispensary.

As he moved on, we waited to toast in unison.

Meanwhile, I felt this cold, wet running down my arm and sleeve and I looked down to see a puddle in front of me. In sequence, each of the others went through the same movement, like a choreographed dance line.

That rotgut had dissolved the paper cups!

We walked out of the chateau to listen to the competing German and American caroling.

Then, Lt. Herman said: "Just think, at this moment, the Chaplains on both sides of the line are telling their men that God is on their side!"

Merry Christmas!

HAPPY NEW YEAR!

Lt. Herman was at the opposite pole of the humanity scale from Capt. Wilson.

He was a bone in Wilson's throat because he amiably failed to recognize Wilson's determination to exercise absolute control over everyone. I am sure Wilson was intimidated by the clout Herman had at the Division HQ, an uncle who was a Colonel on the Staff.

Nor, did Wilson appreciate Herman's artless, democratic fraternizing with the staff. Rank was no big issue with Herman.

Herman particularly liked me for some reason, I suppose because we shared some similar quixotic attitudes.

Since I was able to handle some German language, he took me with him to Regimental HQ several times to help with prisoner interrogation.

I sensed a resentment in Whitmore, our jeep driver, on these occasions. I believed at the time that it was a feeling that the well-established pecking order was being violated, but I found out later it was something else.

On the first matter, however, it occurred to me repeatedly during later years, that even some Americans desire a Germanic "Alles in ordnung" (Everything in order) and when class lines or corporate tables of organization are breached, the problems are not so much with the elite, but with the pecked-upon lower level employees, who become very uncomfortable.

I remember, in my one season with the Symphony Orchestra, getting into an animated conversation with our soloist, a world renowned violinist. He enjoyed it enough to correspond with me later, but among my fellow grunts in the orchestra, I had become a pushy pariah who could most likely rape a nun.

Then, on New Year's Eve, Hitler called what he assumed would be a morale builder for his people, but, what was to become a suicidal attack up and down our lines.

In our sector, there was a slaughter of dark uniformed Wehrmacht sharply outlined against the snow covered, moon illuminated fields. It was a crystal clear night on that New Year's Eve on the Saar River.

Lt. Herman brought me a diary taken from one body to seek out military information. It became one of the most painful experiences of my young life.

On the inside of the cover was his photo, a very bland middle-aged face with myopic eyes looking through round wire rimmed glasses under his Wehrmacht soft cap. He looked like an "off the rack" German accountant. Not fierce at all!

On the opposite page was a photo of a pleasantly plain-faced woman with two blonde straight short-haired girls of about eight and ten in front of her.

The text chronicled how, because of his age and poor health, he had been called up only four months before into a unit composed mostly of the aging and the very young, and the mundane things they had been doing since then.

It was the last entry that moved me: He told his wife how much he loved her and the children and how much he missed her personally. He told her that he did not expect to survive this mission and the next time they would meet would be in Heaven.

There was no military information.

There was no "Heil Hitler", just a small crushed down rose.

I put my head down on the table and cried.

Valhalla

In early 1945, we made our move across the Saar River.

The goal was to lay the groundwork for an assault upon the Siegfried Line, the major defensive barrier into the heart of Germany.

It was the first engagement in which we participated as a unit.

We watched as our battalion crossed by small boats to the German-occupied sister town on the other side. Germany was only a few kilometers beyond.

There was only one casualty in the boat crossings, but the enemy snipers had picked off several Company C riflemen as they crossed the stone bridge.

One was still alive and calling for help from the middle of the span after the others ran for cover on the other side.

Sgt. Bruce was their company aid man, and he started for the bridge. Sgt. Adams grabbed his arm: "Wait until they clear the snipers!"

Bruce pushed his hand off. No one was going to abort his first chance for immortality.

He ran off toward the bridge, hitting the span like the half-back he was, swiveling and dodging those tackling bullets like an all-American or like John Wayne on the beaches of Iwo Jima. I think he was mentally reading the press notices he was sure to get, when the final tackler got him, and he fell dead over the goal line on top of the soldier he had gone out to save.

Score: One wounded man with bullet in his thigh.

One dead medic with bullet in his heart.

But, Bruce did get the immortality he sought.

He got a Silver Star posthumously for his valiant effort, a press notice in the hometown paper and his mother got the opportunity to put a gold star in her window.

He also validated my prediction that he would be among the first combat casualties in our outfit. He was actually the first.

FRAGGED

The boys in the Viet Nam war used the term "fragged."

It was a short term for getting rid of dangerous or unpopular officers by throwing grenades into their tents.

During the "Good War" it was: Do the job during hostile fire! I never dreamed, with my humane approach to life, that I would be speaking so casually of murder, but combat changes the rules of the ethical game. It is one's own life that is at stake.

Some leaders in combat are simply dangerous to one's health.

It is one thing to be willing to sacrifice one's life and limb for country in a rational plan with prospects for success. It is an entirely different matter to do so in a plan hatched in the minds of ego-maniacs or morons, be they generals or corporals.

Later in our campaign, one Major, the incompetent executioner of an uncounted number of our boys, was last seen being walked off into the woods by some of our officers. I never saw him again and I never asked where he went.

I mention this now because of that one casualty in the boat crossings. Missouri and Watters picked him up. It was the commander of the first platoon of Company D.

Although we did not know it then, there was no doubt in the minds of the riflemen that he would be one of the first casualties.

Lawson and I helped move him off the litter onto Corporal Walsh's table.

Lawson was shocked: "He's shot in the back!"

Walsh ignored him.

Lawson grabbed his arm. "You didn't hear me! He's shot in the back!"

"So, turn him over!" said Walsh. Then, he looked at us levelly as he was bandage compressing the bleeding wounds.

"If you are smart, you will say nothing about this."

Lawson and I looked at each other. We were puzzled.

I made it a point later to speak with Grossman, the company aid man from Kansas City.

He didn't seem at all upset. "If you're asking me, whether I am sorry he was shot. Yes, I am! If you're asking me whether I was sorry to see him go. No, I'm not. I hope he recovers quickly and has a nice trip home.... permanently."

Then, he told me stories about this officer's disdain for his men and the cultures from which they were drawn, and the events of the past two months, where his men's lives were being risked on numerous patrols of questionable value that could only be interpreted as "glory-seeking."

As ye sow.......

BAPTISM

The Germans withdrew to their own border, which opened up more ground for us on the east side of the Saar River. For the first time our litter bearing teams were free to operate independently.

My own started walking inland along a road bordering a railroad track. About four kilometers inland, a jeep bore down upon us with a badly wounded rifleman.

We put him on a litter and took turns shoulder carrying him in. After about a kilometer, while we were changing carriers, Missouri said: "The guy's dead!"

The four of us looked at each other over the body, then Missouri and Watters hoisted him again and we continued our trek to the aid station.

Whitmore and Corporal Fitzpatrick, another of our aid station technicians, were bearing down upon us in our jeep. They got out to help load the casualty for the trip back.

Fitzpatrick looked down: "You assholes! This guy's dead!"

We stood looking at him: "Like, so what?"

"Don't ever waste your energy on a dead man!" He grabbed the side of the litter and dumped the body face down at the side of the road. "Go find somebody you can help!" He jumped back into the jeep and they roared off.

We stood looking at each other.

Every litter bearer goes through this baptism. It goes against every grain in our own natures to abandon a fellow American, a fellow soldier, even though he is dead.

But we must, in order to move on and help the living.

It was a painful lesson, and we never did it again.

We picked up our litters and moved on.

MUSINGS

Many books have been written about the absurdities of war.

I just want to give my own impressions.

Our first engagement demonstrates it all.

We watched our boys cross the Saar river. We recognized them as individuals who had been loved, schooled, given cod liver oil, medical attention, orthodontia, psychologists and all the other help in growing up.

They go across the river, and no matter whether they were sinners or saints, morons or geniuses, they go into the same meat grinder and some come streaming back through our aid station for repairs.

Those who died, no longer count. They are just bagged and shipped home, and the next batch goes into the meat grinder.

The idea of doctors standing at the butcher shop tables, waiting to repair the human meat and bones they know are being deliberately ground up on the other side of the river, boggles me.

The ultimate absurdity were the German casualties. On their side of the river we were trying like hell to kill them; on our side of the river, we were trying like hell to save them.

One needs to pull the discs of rationality and sanity out of one's mental computer or risk blowing the fuses.

One needs to mindlessly accept these absurd terms and play by the macabre rules of this game in order to emotionally survive the psychological and ethical savaging.

DEFENDER OF THE FAITH

We got back to our little apartment opposite the aid station at dark. I crawled into my sleeping bag. I was white with exhaustion and feeling lousy.

At about three in the morning, Sgt. Adams awakened us. Night fighting had broken out at the lines, and we were needed.

I tried to get out of my sleeping bag, but couldn't. I was drenched with sweat. Adams felt my forehead, realized I was really sick, and took off with the other guys. I popped some aspirins.

At dawn, I felt guilty. The other guys were out there in danger without me. I took my temperature. It was 103 degrees. I took some more aspirins and dropped off again.

I would awaken at intervals when I heard jeeps and ambulances pulling up to the aid station. I felt very, very guilty and dropped off again.

At ten AM, I dragged myself out of the sack and took my temperature. It was 101 and I smelled like a horse blanket, so I stripped off my clothes and put dry underwear on.

After I dressed, I staggered down the stairs and over to the aid station. There was a mess inside. Everyone was busy.

I went over to Walsh's table. He seemed pleased to have my help and I did all right for a while, then, as had been my running bad luck, the stripping of clothing off of some very savage wounds coincided with my next bout of dizziness, and I felt like I was passing out.

As I discovered again and again, most people put the spin upon events that conform to their expectations and prejudices and not the truth. Walsh, with a tone of dripping contempt, shouted over to Peters, "Come over here and help me! The kid, here, can't stand the sight of blood."

I tried to explain that I was ill, but he waved me away as Peters took my spot at the table. I realized that the matter was moot as far as he was concerned, so I quietly slipped out of the door.

GIVE ME THAT OLD TIME RELIGION

My experience with Corporal Peters was much more gratifying.

He was an aid station technician, a Southern Baptist farm boy from South Carolina, good hearted, fair-minded, although, not really very bright. I really resented some of the arrogant others referring to him privately as "white trash." And, I was very vocal about condemning them for their bigotry. Although, that did not sit well with these guys, I was on his side and I believe that he sensed that.

While I sat on the stoop outside, trying to stop my head from spinning and force back the nausea, he tapped me on the shoulder as he passed: "It's hell out there! We've got to go!"

Whitmore whipped the jeep around the corner and we hopped in. I discovered that under stress our bodies are often able to rise to the challenge and the flu symptoms were fading quickly.

The battle had narrowed into a wooded area about one kilometer from the aid station. Whitmore got as close on the road as he was able. Peters grabbed a litter and ran into the woods with me following.

As loud as the fire fighting had sounded outside of the woods, it was horrendous within. Putrid gun smoke fumes floated in horizontal layers. I could sense bullets passing me and hear them ricocheting off of trees. It was like being inside of a huge church with the organ playing percussion at maximum volume.

I didn't know which way death was coming from and stood frozen waiting for it to strike.

Peters dropped the litter next to a wounded rifleman and rolled the man on. Since voice contact was decibels out of reach, he pointed for me to pick up the head end. That was a mistake. It was the heavier end and I had to walk backwards.

I felt the handles slipping out of my fingers and as I tried to readjust positions, I tripped over a communication wire and the poor wounded guy screamed loud enough to be heard over the sounds of that hell as his head and the litter landed in my lap.

I could see by the surprised look on Peter's face that he might certify Walsh's evaluation of my courage. He dragged the patient-laden litter off my legs. Bruises and all, I painfully rose.

"Please, God!" I prayed. "I know that you know that I don't really think you're up there. But, if you are, give this skinny little guy the strength to match this other guy and the courage to prevail."

Strangely, a bubble of calm seemed to surround us, blocking out bullets, shrapnel and noise. I walked to the foot of the litter and nodded to Peters to lift.

I can't say that I did not believe my arms would be pulled out of their sockets, nor that my hands would have tendinitis for the rest of my life, but I did prevail. We went back into the jaws of death three more times.

As we watched the jeep take off with its last load, Peters turned and pushed my aching shoulder: "You done OK, kid!"

A Congressional Medal of Honor could not have pleased me more!

Although I was still unable to allay my aversion to those who piously wreak havoc with their religions, I was able to take the last step up to theism and from that day forward never denied the existence of a God again.

SANCHO-PANZA

An unlikely alliance arose between Corporal Peters and me. He became sort of a Sancho-Panza to me, the quintessence of folk simplicity. We recognized in the other what we lacked in ourselves.

He had the physical strength I didn't, and I had the imagination he didn't.

There are a variety of skills that we are called upon to exercise by the chance of our cultural environment. Great physical strength was an attribute remotely needed in my normal environment, but in Peter's rural world, it was a primary need.

He inherited the sturdy body of his settler forbearers who survived generations of exhausting rural efforts, while I inherited the body of untold years of city dwellers.

Yet, here we were, together, assigned by fate to the same job.

His cultural skills fascinated me. They were so removed from my own experience. His ability to take a primitive environment and make it livable was uncanny. There was no one who could convert a foxhole into "Home Sweet Home" faster and better than he.

He could take the crappiest food the Army could give us, go into a farm and "liberate" enough ingredients to create a family feast.

His religion was simple and fair. He didn't believe I was going to hell, he just felt obligated to try to save me from it.

Since I have never had any formal religious affiliation, I felt no compunctions about attending chapel services with him, and he was delighted.

That classically trained tenor singing lead on "Onward Christian Soldiers" was me. Peters never really believed that I had embraced the faith, but he believed there was hope, and that was enough for him.

This sturdy son of the South enjoyed pulling the leg of this skinny urban refugee: "Whitey, I know you think I don't like you, but I want you to know I stuck up for you!"

"How's that Peters?"

"Well, they said you wuzn't fit to live with pigs and I said, Oh! Yes you wuz!"

"Thanks, Peters!"

FRATERNIZING

We were having our first direct contact with the German people. The following is an excerpt from the only really despairing letter I ever wrote home:

"You have no idea of the problems that face the world with this Germany. The minds of these people are distorted beyond reasoning.

"One of the guys asked a German man why he hated the Russians. He said the Germans and the English and the Americans are of the same blood, but the Russians are beasts because they are not.

"So this American said: `I'm an American and my parents are from Russia and Poland.' That didn't stop this German one bit. He says what saves America is that there are so many loyal Germans there.

"So this guy answers: `Then, explain General Eisenhower, he's German-American and he hates you!'

"That didn't stop the German, either: `He probably has Jewish blood in him!'

"How are we to deal with such people? They were even told we would butcher them when we arrive.

"Oh, well!"

G.I. Bill

The next day we were able to move the aid station about 10 kilometers across the Saar River. Lt. Herman had been able to ferret out a great location on the main road.

After we were set up, I was able to catch up on the Stars and Stripes, our daily Army newspaper, and found an item about a new veteran's benefit bill Congress had passed which included provisions to underwrite college education.

Nothing was ever a greater boon to the United States than that provision. It reformed college from a playtime for the rich and a haven for scholarship nerds to a broad educational base for the spectacular growth of this country after WW II.

For the first time, I felt the desire to go to college if I could survive this hell.

I was so exited that I went to tell Lt. Herman. As I opened my mouth it sounded as if we were in the interior of a base drum, and plaster began falling from the ceiling.

We thought we had been hit, but when we ran out onto the street we found a battery of 155 mm Howitzers had been set up behind our house and had opened up at the enemy.

Captain Wilson was jumping up and down shouting at the officer in charge, who obviously had plugs in his ears.

Finally, he had his attention. The artillery captain appeared very abashed and the battery went off with its tail between its legs.

Boobs

"Booby traps" were well named. They were intended to be attractive to Boobs.

Land mines to an extent, were predictable. One could guess the logical places where they might be buried.

But no one could ever guess what potential souvenir or artifact would be explosive.

Since, I am not, nor ever was acquisitive, I was at very low risk, but many who considered themselves obligated to relieve the enemy of his pelf, found their paths to eternity paved with Leica cameras, army field glasses, German helmets, rifles, bayonets, et cetera.

Detroit was a compulsive "liberator," but he eschewed small stuff. The next day he decided to explore a three story building across from our aid station.

Suddenly, there was this earthshaking explosion and a cloud of dust enveloped the street.

Detroit, on the third floor, had opened a door into the adjoining building which now had crumbled into a pile of stones about five feet high.

Detroit stood in the third floor door jamb covered with dust, the door still swinging to and fro from the handle he still held.

Later, he wanted to take the door along as a memento, but we wouldn't let him.

THE RAT RACE

The Germans were withdrawing for a major defense at the Siegfried Line and fire fights became more chance encounters than planned resistance, but when they did occur they were nasty.

Whereas one unit would be moving along smoothly, adjoining units on either side might be snagged into nasty battles. Our battalion, now provided with trucks, had been moving along so smoothly that we had deceived ourself into thinking that the end was near.

Lawson and I would be hanging out of the truck singing, "Pore Hans is daid!" which was a parody of the song, "Pore Jud is Daid," from the musical, "Oklahoma!" every time we spotted a German corpse, and even degenerated to the macabre: "Pore Hans is flat!" when we spotted one that had lain in the path of a tank advance. (You must remember, however, we had just turned 19.)

Then, we hit the "battle of the quarry."

If the Major, the battalion commander, had not been such a nut, this would not have become the tragedy it did.

The Germans had holed up in granite crevices and caves.

Instead of calling in the artillery, air strikes or napalm, the Major decided to make a "name" for himself by having his boys go in and clean them out.

By the time our squad had reached there with litters, the "boys" had become as imprisoned in the crevices as the Germans in a madhouse of ricochetting bullets and marble chips. There were as many casualties from the flying chips as bullets.

The four of us stood completely boggled as we watched the Major stalking about like a neurotic Groucho Marx in the makeshift battalion headquarters in one of the caves.

Captain Barker was canceling the Major's absurd orders as fast as he was issuing them. Barker, whose company was trapped in the bowels of the quarry, seemed to be the only one able to keep the Major contained. Perhaps that was because Barker was the nephew of the commanding general.

Upon such a madmen the lives of innocent riflemen depend, I thought.

Barker turned to us. "Guys, I hate to ask you this, because I know it is not your job. One of my boys....a sergeant.....he is very popular with the men....and he has been dead over there overnight. It is really demoralizing my guys. Could you get him out for me? You are really not in a line of fire."

It was not a direct order, nor need we have obeyed it, since we were forbidden to handle the dead, but the pleading edge of his voice moved us. We did his bidding.

The Sergeant had been killed in a sitting position at a 30 caliber machine gun and rigor mortis had already set in, so that when we went to put him on the litter, we had to sit him down and then roll him onto his back.

His men were looking off absently in every other direction, as if all of this was a fantasy, not really happening.

When we put the litter down on the back of the jeep, I was stunned when the body rolled back into a sitting position and his clenched fist hit me in the eye. It is not programmed in one's mind to expect a corpse to spar with one. I was utterly unhinged.

Missouri could not resist the ad lib: "You'll be famous, Whitey! The first man in the Seventh Army to be attacked by a corpse."

In that "Disneyland," it somehow didn't strike me as being unusual at all.

THE UNIVERSAL INSTRUMENT OF LOVE

In the aftermath of the "battle of the stone quarry," casualties from both sides were streaming into our aid station.

As was our policy, seriously wounded Americans were treated first, then seriously wounded Germans, then the lighter wounds, Americans first.

At the very end of the line was this blonde, straight haired, ruddy complexioned young German, who was lying on the floor in the corner, a victim of some mortar fragments.

Cpl. Walsh, dogged tired, led several of us over to him and kneeled down to examine.

We cut off his jacket and shirt and sure enough, in addition to his face, he had a load of these little craters across his front each about three-eighths of an inch across, pooled with blood, none too deep, none life threatening.

We were putting sulfa in each crater and covering them with bandages, when the Captain Wilson walked over. "Serious?" he asked.

"No, Sir!"

Cpl. Walsh had meanwhile pulled down the combat pants and was cutting away the undershorts. Suddenly, he looked up.

"Not serious doctor, but fatal" Then, he spread the underwear.

We all grimaced! The penis had been sliced neatly across the middle and the lower half was hanging by a piece of skin.

The German boy, lifted himself onto his elbows, looked and fell back with a "Mein Gott!"

Detroit was wringing his hands: "Can you do anything, Doctor?"

Wilson shook his head: "Well there's one little batch of Germans that won't be born! Cut it off Walsh, and send him off." He turned and left.

This was something that superseded nation, race or politics. A wave of empathy swept around the congregated.

Walsh pulled out a scissors and got up on his knees, poised. The potential pain radiated out to all of us.

Then he hesitated, sat back on his calves and contemplated. He put the scissors down, poured sulfa on both open ends, joined them, ran a tongue depressor as a splint along the side, and then wrapped tenderly with sterile gauze.

He was acting for all mankind.

He got up, threw a blanket over the boy, and said: "Take him back to the field hospital. Maybe, there is some doctor there who can perform miracles."

We all knew in our hearts that this was an idle hope, but we sure appreciated the effort.

MERCY OR MURDER?

During our twelve hour litter bearing ordeal, we were simply walking along the battle lines, picking up wounded that we were certain were accumulating there.

At C Company, we were told that there was a rifleman lying on the rise behind them. Detroit and I picked our way back to the hillock.

Their company aid man, Sgt. Miles, had just gotten there.

Miles, by any standards, was a strange duck. He was small, at least 36 years old, prematurely grayed and closer to five feet tall than five and a half.

In the few times I had seen him, he was in constant motion, including his mouth, and was famous for his imaginative, exaggerated, but interesting bull shit. Many thought he was a mental case.

In combat, he was everywhere, defying my predictions of early death for such. Perhaps he survived unscathed because he was such a small target and was not doing it to become a hero, although I do remember him becoming the most decorated of the company aid men.

My last memory of him is a photo in a book about the WW II where he is standing knee deep in bodies on a flat bed rail car at Dachau, in the midst of action, as always.

The wounded man was on his face at a forty five degree angle up the rise. We began helping Miles pick away at the shredded combat jacket and shirt. Then we gasped.

In the bright moonlight, we could see that we had also pulled away most of his back. We were looking down into what was left of the tissue and were seeing some bone. We were too exhausted to throw up. "We better get the jeep."

Detroit took off to try to find the company radio man.

I stood up and stayed.

The man was still alive and moaning and Miles was pricking morphine tube needles into his arm. I remember thinking, how will this ever all grow back?

Adding 62 years to Miles age of 36 or so, he is probably passed on by now or I wouldn't tell the rest.

During the next round of heavy shelling, he quickly pulled out a small caliber pistol he has been known to carry for protection in defiance of the Geneva Convention, and directed three bullets into the still pumping heart through the shredded back. Then, just as quickly, the pistol was back into his jacket.

He rotated and fell back in a seated position against the hillock. In the very dim light of the flares and the moon, he realized I was still there. Our eyes locked.

I am sure both of our jaws were dropped.

Detroit came back: "I couldn't find the radio man."

Miles looked up: "It's just as well. He's dead!"

Detroit put his hand on Miles's shoulder: "Don't feel too bad. I don't think he would have made it, anyway."

Then, there was a another burst of heavy fire and the now common cry: "Medic!"

We moved on.

SELECTIVE CATASTROPHES

When we dragged ourselves dirty and exhausted to our billet in mid-morning of the next day, we found Fitzpatrick clean and slick, jet black hair combed straight back and a white silk scarf tucked into his shirt, wheeling up and down the street on a "liberated" bicycle. He could have been a double for a young Victor Mature.

As often occurs in catastrophes such as tornados and hurricanes, damage is selective. While we were going through the most destructive experience to date in our combat involvement, Fitzpatrick had been assigned to an outfit that simply lay on their backs that night looking at the full moon and the stars.

Some of the guys were trying to tell him what we had been through that night and he simply looked at us blankly.

I realized then, that no words, expressed orally or in print, could ever duplicate kinetic experience and involvement. Even movies and sound tracks are mono-directional.

What bothered me was, I was deeply and unfairly resenting his virginal status.

When I slipped in my sleeping bag, despite almost total exhaustion, I was unable to sleep. What Miles had done filled my mind.

A devout Catholic, he was playing God! In this case, I agree, the man's chances at survival were virtually nil, but in how many cases were this particular medical technician's prognoses wrong? If there is a God, how many lives did he end before God intended?

Why didn't he let his God make the final decision?

I decided there was nothing I could do about this. It would be the word of a litter bearer versus an aidman.

I rolled over and went to sleep and didn't even think about it again until after the war.

SENTENCE WITHOUT TRIAL

When I awoke, I had a surprise. Texas's bed roll and all of his equipment, were gone.

Texas, being too young to be shipped over as a replacement from our Texas training camp, had also been assigned to this medical detachment.

Since he was in another litter bearer squad, my contact with him had been limited. I had long since forgiven him for the suspected theft of my watch, and, in fact had come to the conclusion that his conduct was due more to a limited intelligence than evil intent. This latter conclusion was supported by the fact that he simply was not learning the necessary battlefield treatment course being crammed into us by Sgt. Shapiro.

Whether it was his being too dumb, or some other irritant for Captain Wilson, he was sent out to replace a Company aidman casualty.

Sgt. Adams was very disturbed that Company D was being short changed by the assignment of an untrained incompetent.

Sgt. Shapiro was disturbed, because this was the second time the captain's pique had dictated breaking the unwritten code, "Trained aidmen, replace lost company aidmen; litter bearers replace lost litter bearers." Wilson had already sent out another litter bearer, Evans, whose confused mind soon assured his early demise.

We were also coming to the conclusion that he was protecting his favorites, especially Sgt. Fitzpatrick, with whom he had become chummy and his "court jester," Missouri and his shadow, Watters.

Shapiro warned me again, "Stay away from that guy!"

CHICKEN

A truism had formed in my mind: There is no way of predicting how a parade field soldier will react in combat.

Some, like Sgt. Adams, excelled in both.

At one extreme there were those, like Missouri, who were excellent in non-combat soldiering and cowards under fire.

At the other extreme, like ex-fly boy Lerner, they were non-combat disasters and combat "legends."

First Sergeant Wagner, arguably an excellent barracks soldier albeit an SOB, himself resolved the debate over whether his depression withdrawal was the trauma of leaving his wife or cowardice. The consensus opinion had been the latter.

We were so accustomed to seeing him sitting around noiselessly while mayhem circulated about him, that we were surprised when he wandered over and watched the aid room action of the "night of hell."

Soon, he picked up some bandages and began to help. It was like he was coming back through a dense fog.

When he began to realize how badly this night was developing, he grabbed a litter and teamed up with Dutch for the rest of the twelve hour marathon, one for which we were all later decorated.

The resurrection was amazing. Wagner was turning into a warm and caring human being.

It is difficult to convey to someone who has not been in the life and death dynamics of combat, the powers that officers and non-coms have over the bodies that have been assigned to them.

Sometimes, intelligent, well educated men of good will are endangered by ignorant, incompetent, sometimes semi-literate, or brutal leadership. Wagner's transformation was like a miracle.

Since, there was no possibility of his resuming his former responsibilities, he volunteered to join a company as an aid man, probably the only first sergeant in the U.S. Army history to serve in that capacity.

Meanwhile, Lerner, who had become our battalion ambulance driver, was wheeling around all over the place and becoming a legend. He was a lone wolf who refused a second driver, and was even known to roll onto the field of battle itself, bypassing the litter bearers for casualties.

His life now seemed to have regained purpose.

Lawson and I were confirming our suspicions that Missouri and his shadow, Watters, were cowards. We realized, that despite carrying many casualties and regaling Capt. Wilson about their "heroic" deeds, they had somehow avoided actually being exposed to direct fire. Somehow the most dangerous assignments had fallen exclusively to Lawson and me. This uneven distribution of risk was more than simple chance.

When I asked Sgt. Adams to assign Lawson our team leadership, he shook his head knowingly. There was no chance of that so long a Missouri was Captain Wilson's pet.

Missouri was certainly destined to become an excellent middle-management politician.

THE PREACHER

In the case of Sgt. Adams, it was our evaluation of him that changed, not his conduct.

Despised because of his "chicken shit" repression in the States, he became highly admired for his grace in combat.

He never asked us to go where he wouldn't lead.

He was eminently fair in his distribution of dangerous assignments, and fiercely protective of our safety in the hands of even our most moronic officers.

As I said, he looked, talked and acted like Harry Truman, without the profanities, of course.

An unusual relationship grew up between this Methodist minister from a small town in Wisconsin and this Chicago agnostic.

My most endearing memory is the day we walked into a wooded area to pick up some casualties, Sgt. Adams in the lead of course. As almost always, I was walking by his side.

Suddenly, he stopped, looked at me fiercely through his wire rimmed glasses, and said: "Walk behind me, Whitey!"

I was bewildered at this unexpected display of regressive behavior.

Then, he turned to the others and barked: "Get in single file the way you were taught, and increase the intervals! I don't want to see a single one of you out of line!"

Chicken shit, again!

When, we got to the edge of the woods, he waited for all of us to catch up.

He turned to my obviously disappointed face: "We just walked through a mine field!"

Sure enough, when I looked back closely at the plowed field, I could see the edges of what were called "shoe box mines" designed only to blow off feet. Archer, not wanting any of us to become alarmed into starting a fatal stampede had myopically led our way through a mine field at least one city block square.

There is a tragic aftermath to this story.

On our way out of the woods bearing the wounded on our shoulders, we came upon a macabre scene on the mine field that demonstrated the mindlessness that is so common in combat.

A soldier walking through the same mine field had blown a foot off. A comrade rushed out to help him and blew his foot off. Two others in a jeep drove out to help both and blew a tire. One of these panicked, jumped out of the jeep to run back, blew his foot off and fell onto other mines which exploded and killed him. The last soldier was screaming for help and looked as if he were going to jump out and run, also.

Adams pointed at him and in his strongest Charlton Heston voice commanded him to sit down.

No one was going to argue with Moses. He did!

Then, Preacher Adams turned to the 90-day wonder commanding the platoon and instructed: "Have your messenger call in a tank and get them out!"

"Yes, Sir!" said the Lieutenant, saluting a sergeant, and Moses turned and led his children out of the Valley of Death.

PISTOLS

Of all the souvenirs eagerly sought by American "liberators", European handguns wreaked the most mischief.

Riflemen, who were superb with their native weapon, were imbecilic with handguns.

At first, there was a suspicion that self-inflicted wounds of the extremities were only techniques for getting off of the firing line, but when these wounds continued after hostilities ceased, it was a foretelling of the hand gun insanity that plagues our country to this day, courtesy of the National Rifle Association.

Even I, who considered himself expert with the handgun, left a bullet in the chamber of one that a rifleman was showing me while I was toying around with the hammer. The bullet went through two walls and into an outhouse, where, thankfully, another rifleman was in a sitting position.

One soldier will never have children after shoving a Luger into the front of his belt. Another will have a permanent slice out of one buttock when he jammed a Belgian P-38 into the back of his belt. There are those who will limp for life and some who are no longer with us after showing off their trophies.

Then, for some inexplicable reason, a civilian insisted on surrendering to me a Walther automatic (the kind 007 James Bond uses) virginally fresh in it's box. Since, it is suicide for a medic to be caught with a pistol, I hid it away in my bedroll until the time we were given three days of R&R in a house in a small village.

Peters was hard at work collecting ingredients for one of his family meals from the barn behind the house.

We were all shiny and clean after our showers and were sporting new uniform and underwear issues.

When Peters decided to add chicken to the stew, I pleaded with him to let me try out my new pistol toy.

Then, I took careful aim at the fowl who looking at me curiously out of one eye in the back yard while the whole group watched from the sidelines.

The shot went off, the chicken went straight up into the air, feathers went flying everywhere and we began the chase around the barnyard.

Everyone was scattering and hiding behind wagons and sheds.

I was running out of bullets, but luckily the chicken got her head caught between the barn wall and a ladder and, impaled there, was watching me approach her with great determination.

I aimed very, very carefully and pulled the trigger. A cloud of dust came down off of the barn wall.

The chicken was still looking at me curiously.

Peters was disgusted, so he did a South Carolina chicken-flip with the poor chicken's neck and went into the house.

I realized immediately that I had been functioning across the grain of my culture and nature. I was an excellent shot at non-living targets. I just didn't want to hit that chicken.

I gave away the pistol to a rifleman that very afternoon.

As I have often said since, liberated hand guns should have been named "Hitler's revenge!"

G.I. BILL REVISITED

I was standing in front of Lt. Herman in this doctor's building we had appropriated for an aid station.

He was sitting behind the doctor's desk in the corner of the room flanked by two windows, looking dapper as usual, his trademark white aviator's scarf around his neck, pouring over his ubiquitous maps.

Three other litter bearers were sprawled out on some of the hospital cots on the second floor.

"Lt. Herman, I have been trying to tell you something for the last month and something happens each time!"

I was referring to the Stars and Stripes item about a G.I. Bill of Rights which included assistance in attending college. I was quite excited about the prospect of being able to afford higher education.

If you remember, the first time I started to tell him, an ear busting roar from a battery of 155 mm Howitzers set up behind our building interrupted me.

On the second try, we were thrown ass over heads by the beginning of a tank attack.

This time I was determined.

"Go ahead, Whitey....get it over with!"

I opened my mouth.....a horrible explosion! A German shell hit the corner of the building behind Herman. Glass, dust and debris blew in through the flanking windows. We could hear our boys upstairs rolling down the stairs.

The dust subsided while we, frozen in time, continued to look at each other. Impeccable Herman looked as if he was being prepared for a plaster casting.

"I don't know what you were trying to tell me, Whitey, but whatever it was, don't try again!"

I never did!

God's Numbering System

I have been asked how one begins to accept the risk of death, and walk erect and seemingly fearlessly through combat.

I can only use the analogy of a person having a missile thrown at his body. He would employ evasive maneuvers. If from two or three directions simultaneously, maneuvering might still be successful.

But, when twenty or more missiles come at you from all different directions including above, you give up dodging or hiding. It has now grown beyond your powers to evade, so you resume normal patterns and become fatalistic.

However, I was not superstitious like the other guys who would say: "If that bullet has my number on it, I'll get it. Otherwise, I'll know, God doesn't want to rush me back up there."

Death at times is very selective.

I remember three instances, vividly.

First, Sgt. Adams and I were walking back through a wooded area, our unit having just been relieved by the Third Battalion, which, through a freak of rotation, had never been previously committed to combat.

At the first enemy resistance, the entire Third Battalion went into full retreat right through us, with their officers chasing after them shooting pistols and carbines into the air.

Our boys dropped down and began setting up resistance against the Germans again, who were now breaking through the trees right behind the retreating battalion.

Adams and I dropped on either side of one of the riflemen, scared shitless at this turn of events.

We heard the rumble of this German tank and we could see the top of its turret as it moved up the culvert toward us.

Then, the turret carrying its deadly 88 millimeter gun swung slowly down to point right at us. The loosened dirt began to give way under it, and the tank began sliding slowly back into the culvert. By the time the 88 was fired, it hit a tree behind us showering shrapnel down that was bouncing off of our helmets.

"I can't believe it," I said.

"God was with us," said Adams.

Later, I tapped the rifleman on the back and said, "OK to get up now, guy!"

He didn't move. Adams bent down and took his helmet off. He looked up at me. Then, he turned the helmet over and emptied it.

The shrapnel that had showered on us harmlessly, had cleaned his brain pan out, and left us unscathed on either side.

Another time, I and several others were standing in a wooded area discussing procedures face-to-face with several officers. The messenger was standing at the end of the line looking at all of us.

A sniper shot rang out. Because of the neat rows that German's employ when they reforest, the bullet sped right down that old alley, between all of us and the messenger dropped like a fallen log at our feet.

If we had been standing one foot one way or the other......

The pivotal point in my march to fatalism occurred one evening when I was walking on a road cut out of the side of a small mountain in the Black Forest.

A single German shell looped over the mountain to what seemed like inches over my head to hit on the side below me, showering the shrapnel outward and up.

The angle of the mountain protected me.

The explosion was so formidable, however, that it knocked me head over heels into semi-consciousness.

As I said, I'm not superstitious, but if that shrapnel had my number on it........

IMMORTALITY

On the other hand, one must not permit a sense of fatalism to slip into a sense of immortality.

Oftentimes, when one has survived in the face death a number of times, one can come to assume that there is nothing out there with your number on it.

In that case, one stops assessing the potential consequences of his action, while there are time and options still available.

The worst consequence of that state of mind that I ever witnessed was on a day when we were unable to dislodge a German unit from a wooded area.

A line of ten American tanks came rumbling down the bordering road on the way to a mission. The lead tank was under a First Sergeant who stopped and asked about the problem.

He got down off the tank. "We can take care of that for you in no time, can't we, boys?"

The skinny young medic with the red cross on his helmet and eleven weeks of anti-tank training broke into the officer confab saying: "I don't know sergeant, I think I heard anti-tank weaponry in there."

I got the withering "who the hell do you think you are, private?" look.

The tank sergeant gave us his immortality pitch: "We have eighteen tanks in our whole unit, have been operation in Germany for months and never lost a single one in action!"

He got back on his tank and they all pivoted and crashed into the woods running over trees and shrubbery into the interior.

There was a horrendous exchange of gunfire and in about fifteen minutes the sergeant and bunch of his men came running out of the shrubbery on foot. The rest were casualties of some sort. Seven tanks out of ten tanks were destroyed.

They were unable to maneuver in the wooded area, and they were sitting ducks for the German anti-tank and 88 weaponry.

So much for the "immortality syndrome!"

HEROISM

Of the three battalion aid stations, it was very clear to all that ours was the best in the Regiment.

The quality of the station derives directly from the quality of the doctor, and ours was a crackerjack.

The Second Battalion aid station had a sad sack doctor, so it ended up being called "the fuck up station" and we pitied any casualty that was routed through. The litter bearers were wimps who mostly hid out in foxholes.

The Third Battalion station fell somewhere between.

This was brought to mind some years later when my wife and I were invited to the home of an old friend we had not seen in years. We were anxious to meet her husband and children.

During dinner one of the little boys said: "You know my daddy was a war hero!" The father pooh-poohed and exhibited modesty.

"He was a lieutenant!"

"Really?"

Father: "Well I was really a medical administrative officer."

"Where?"

"Well, in Europe during 1944 and 45," he said softly and modestly.

"So was I! What Army?"

"The Seventh."

It turned out he was in the same Division, also.

He started getting very nervous as I was narrowing down to the Battalion.

"And, he got lots of medals. Tell him about the medals, dad!"

By now, the father was very nervous and looked as if he were about to pass out.

I sat with hand in chin looking at him with squinted eyes trying to place him in my memory.... Years, after all, had changed us all.

Then I remembered. He was no officer. He had been one of the "fuck up" litter bearers with the second battalion aid station.

As recognition crossed my countenance, I saw a look of pleading unrivalled in my experience. His eyes were screaming: "Please!"

My face went blank. "Well, I am sorry, I really didn't know anybody in the other battalions." I went back to eating dinner. His eyes were screaming: "Thank you!"

The moral is: Don't tell stories until you are sure that every living witness in the Universe is dead!

The Million Dollar Wound

We were losing Company aid men with great regularity, now. As I mentioned, combat medics have the highest casualty rate.

They felt that they lived in misery and that we lived in luxury and on a relative scale they were right. As miserable as our conditions were, theirs were unfailingly worse. After all, we had the luxury of getting away from hundreds of yards to many kilometers the lines.

As Einstein said: "All things are relative!"

I particularly remember Larson. He was tall, well educated and one of the "fly boys." In contrast with the others, he was unfailingly gracious and never complained about the cruel turn of fate they had endured.

One very dark, miserable, rainy night during a lull in a two day foxhole to foxhole engagement, we were called out to Company A where he was the medic.

We arrived there in time to see a company sergeant holding a gun on Larson demanding that he go over the barbed wire into no man's land to do something for a rifleman who was begging for help after stepping on a land mine.

Larson finally said: "You might as well shoot. I might as well die here as in that mine field." I had the feeling the sergeant would shoot. His and everyone else's nerves were going after hearing an old comrade begging all night for help.

Lawson spoke up. It surprised me. He was well bred, normally not outspoken: "I'll tell you what Sergeant, if you go with us, we'll go out and bring him in for you." I couldn't really see that well in the dark, but I was reaching for Lawson's throat.

There was a silence, then the Sergeant dropped the muzzle of his gun and walked away.

"Thanks, guys!" said Larson.

I grabbed Lawson by the shoulders: "You would really go out there?"

"I lied," he said simply.

When we did lose a company aid man, if he died we never saw him again. If he was wounded he would generally come through our aid station.

One day, I found Larson, sitting on one of the tables in the aid station, happy as a clam. I had never seen him so smiling and elated.

His right leg was bandaged to the knee.

"Is it bad?" I asked him.

"Terrible!" he said smiling, "I'll never be able to walk well again!"

"So what the hell are you so happy about?"

"Compared to what I though would get, this is a "million dollar" wound! I'm going home! I hope you're this lucky, you bastard!"

As Einstein said: "All things are relative."

THE CHAPLAIN

The Protestant Chaplain and his driver were two of our most favorite people.

He had been the Pastor of a socially prominent Presbyterian church on the North Shore of Long Island.

His driver was a handsome, dignified, grey haired former executive of a major national radio network in New York City.

Their unfailing good humor could only be described as elegant, and in the most somber of times and in the most dangerous of situations, they could be depended upon to wheel up and spread their good cheer.

We were devastated when we learned that in wheeling out to another dangerous area where they felt their services would be needed, their jeep hit a land mine that was designed for a tank.

I remember, when I joked with them that they should be put in for combat decorations, the Chaplain joked back: "We are only interested in decorations given out by the Lord."

I am certain, St. Peter must have pinned a bunch of them on these boys when they arrived.

PIG ALLEY

"Pig Alley" was the G.I.'s mispronunciation of the Parisian red light district, Pig Alley.

With the Louvre, Versailles, Eiffel Tower, Bastille and other sights that romantics yearn to visit, all I would hear from most of the boys in our outfit who won passes to Paris was about Pig Alley.

Of all things, Missouri was number one in the lottery for passes and he and Detroit were the first to go.

When they returned, while Missouri was regaling the assembled about all the big boobs, wiggling asses and "Couche avec mois?" Detroit drew me aside and asked: "Do you want to know why I call it Pig Alley? Because that's were all the pigs are who are wearing the inserts to our combat jackets!"

I was outraged!

To understand why, one would need to know that it was realized early on that fighting in Army overcoats was simply too clumsy. So, we were issued what were called, "combat jackets," which were loosely fitted so that in really cold weather we could wear tight fitting fur-lined inserts.

The problem was that when winter hit, these inserts never arrived. That is, a handful did come, but the bulk of the requisition never made it to the front. Every time we received new supplies, we searched for them but found nothing.

Meanwhile most of the guys were freezing their asses off in the foxholes. It was so serious that the instructions to graves registration and to us was not to send back these inserts with the dead or wounded if they were salvageable for redistribution to the other riflemen. Sometimes, if the insert arms were bloody or shredded we would cut them down and give them to a lineman.

If I sound angry, I still am to this day.

The absurdity of our form of warfare was that there were a great number of support people who lived in relative comfort in the rear areas, or in the States, while a comparative few were actually interfaced with the enemy in combat in generally lousy weather conditions.

When rear area supply people spotted "gonad grabbers" like these body fitting inserts that, incidentally, made anybody look like Charles Atlas, they grabbed one for themselves, one for their buddy, one for their buddy's buddy and so on until it was estimated that there were about 250,000 of these combat-needed inserts wafting around on sex missions in Paris alone.

Much of our best food rations got short stopped for the mademoiselles, also.

In the struggle between gonads and morality, gonads win.

Detroit told Lt. Herman, who told Captain Coburn (who was the nephew of a general on the staff), who in turn ripped up the supply sergeants, and finally our shipments began to arrive in time to miss most of the winter.

If perchance any of the boys who participated in this supply rape of the men who were fighting and dying on the lines read this, I would like them to know that even after sixty-two years, the bitterness lingers on.

Dutch

Dutch was from Grand Rapids, Michigan. I never mentioned him before because he really didn't impact upon us that much. He was just there.

It is difficult to describe his personality, except to say that he was like a great big bear. He was well over 200 pounds, large for those days, and in many ways reminded me of "Lenny" in Steinbeck's "Of Mice and Men." I don't think he had a mean bone in his body, and his most pervasive emotion was fear.....constant and unremitting.

Yet, he never finked out on a dangerous job, and the advantage of working with him is that you were sure to get out of a danger zone at lightening speed.

The one time that our casualty loaded jeep was immobilized in mud tracks, "screaming mimmies" started coming in on us. Dutch grabbed the front end of jeep and turned in on to higher ground and then went around and did likewise to the back. It was a very crude effort and one of the wounded rolled off, but I am sure he was as pleased as we to get the hell out of there!

If he worked a litter with someone who was not near enough his equal in strength, he was just as likely to carry the casualty out by himself.

He was a permanent target of Missouri's low class humor.

One day, we all had to drop behind a low rise in the ground under automatic rifle fire. Trouble was Dutch's ass showed above the rise. He took a nick on a cheek that was no worse than a razor nick on the other cheeks, but, one would have thought he had suffered a mortal wound.

Missouri was trying to convince him that he would never sit properly again, and that he definitely deserved a Purple Heart. Dutch thought that was a great idea and Lt. Herman got one for him.

Two more nicks in other places -- two more purple hearts.

Missouri, in fact all of us, thought this was all hysterical, that is, until we later discovered that each of these medals entitled him to five points toward the one hundred and thirty-eight that one needed to be returned to the States.

These final fifteen points completed his qualification, and he was the first of us to go home.

CHARACTER

I was a very faithful writer of letters home because of my mother's anxieties.

As a matter of fact, I was an upbeat liar, if you want to know the truth, and she rightly never really believed me.

This is one I wrote but never mailed, exactly as written (including lousy punctuation). Please remember, this is a nineteen year old writing in high school prose:

"Only now, as the horror of it all recedes, am I able to realize how much I had learned in those few short months. No one can come out of it unchanged.

"It's all well and good to see the debris and the results after it is done, but seeing it done, that is the lesson.

"For then you can realize how in an instant, one small mistake, one small decision in the mind of a man can change the course of things. One squeeze of the trigger -- a human life, one shell -- a home, perhaps a family.

"What destiny, what hopes, what cherished possession did we unwittingly destroy? What mother's son, what child's father, what hearts did we break?

"One day a Jerry unwittingly walked into our positions. In the brief instant of realization he had two choices, surrender, or escape. He chose escape -- and death. All in a brief instant. He might have been a genius or he might have been a dupe but in that one crucial moment, the one that counted, he made the wrong decision.

"There is something else that combat and only combat troops can experience that can never known by any other type of soldier. The importance of the other fellow. When lives are at stake you finally come to realize the importance of character.

"Following an attack, my buddy and I went out to the outposts and brought back a seriously wounded man on a litter. We were moving back through the woods occupied by the battalion when German tanks broke through and entered the woods with supporting fire from their mortars. Needless to say pandemonium broke loose.

"Those who had holes ran for them and those who had not ran to the rear. Burdened down with the litter, we couldn't run. The only alternative was to leave the patient and dive for cover which wasn't morally in us to do. The din was terrific, shrapnel flying everywhere. We pleaded for help but they heedlessly ran by us and in a few moments we were the only Americans above ground.

"With its 88 roaring, a Tiger tank turned into our neck of the woods. Then, suddenly, two soldiers jumped out of their fox-holes grabbed the litter and together we managed to run through the mortar fire and out of danger. Out of the 800 men in the immediate vicinity only two men had it in them to leave comparative safety of their foxholes to help, as they put it in their own words, 'A couple of right guys that wouldn't leave a buddy.'"

To which I must add, today, those two riflemen are the ones that really had Character.

HAPPINESS IS A WARM FOXHOLE

Something needs to be said about foxholes, the much maligned habitat of the G.I.

The basic foxhole, of course, is a simple grave-like excavation below the firing line.

The hope is that one will emerge like Lazarus, the grave-likeness not withstanding.

Of course, some such are really intended to be "slit trenches," created for other imperative human functions, and the neophyte who confuses the two is likely to need a whole new change of wardrobe, if he survives.

The American instinct is to improve. Therefore, foxholes range from simple, canopy covered models to elaborate underground mansions with drop coverings, Coleman lanterns, candles, tin can stoves, warm bedrolls and general conviviality.

Construction of a foxhole initiates spontaneously upon stopping for latrine purposes, waiting for transportation, or even just a red light.

The hacking of entrenching tools through concrete, asphalt, stone, and hopefully earth, creates a unique cacophony.

But for better or worse, it is home until the next move is made.

Not enough has been said about foxholes as temples of devotion.

I know for a fact that there was much more genuine and heartfelt prayer in the foxholes of the military during WW II than in all the churches and synagogues of the United States and all of its possessions put together.

I, for one, never had to dig a foxhole. Being a medic, I was always a welcome and honored guest in any rifleman's abode. In fact, I needed to be careful to eventually RSVP all invitations without discrimination.

Foxholes for me, in fact, were my first motel experience.

Nothing can match the homeyness of these constructions nor their stress reducing propensities.

When the snow is falling, the winds are howling, and the enemy is lurking, happiness is, indeed, a warm foxhole.

BEDROLLS, JEEPS AND OTHER JOYS

I have never seen homage paid to the Army bedroll.

I am sure it was the forerunner of the American love affair with traveling trailer homes.

Wherever our bedrolls were, that was "home."

Ours would be piled onto one of our company trailer hitches and dragged to our new locations, be it a Chateau, farm house or foxhole.

These had dropped into them whatever we personally possessed, photos, extra socks, souvenirs or even tins of anchovies.

A thoughtless, rapid self-insertion into one of those sometimes smelly envelopes could incur broken toes, but once in, they were like a mother's womb, nourishing, warm and secure.

Combat boots were the forerunner of muscle resistance training. Just moving those clodhoppers, one developed calves like a Walter Payton.

When caked with mud, you walked in them like Frankenstein's monster, but they did give you protection for anything short of having a tank run over your foot.

When I first returned to civilian shoes, I could feel every pebble in the road. I felt as if I were in soft-bottomed moccasins, and muscle memory caused me to kick myself in the chin many a time, trying only to cross my legs.

Zippo lighters were the most ubiquitous piece of non-military hardware we possessed.

They were all function, with no form; ugly little cubes rounded at the top.

They were also unintended military substitutes for worry beads. The ringing sound of tops being opened and snapped shut at the rate of sixty times a minute rings down the years in the memory of 11,000,000 veterans of WW II.

They were great for setting fire to cigarettes, kindling, as well as tips of noses and head hair when overfilled.

Such an overfilled lighter could shoot a flame three feet in the air and guarantee the execution of the soldier who brought down a mortar barrage with his indiscretion.

But they did elicit so much residual affection from the G.I. that they rose from plebeian stainless steel models to solid gold casings after the war.

Not enough can ever be said about the Jeep. All purpose everything, go anywhere, do anything.

We learned very early on that mounting two litters over the back seats was the best hernia preventative ever devised.

But best of all, with chassis belly skimming the mud, it could get us and our casualties rapidly out of the jaws of death.

I don't know of anyone who could really stomach C-rations. The only way they were palatable was if one found some other ingredients to add. The closest I can come to describing the contents is corn beef hash.

One thing was guaranteed. You would slash your fingers on the tin.

K-rations were the aristocrats of concentrated food. They came in boxes.

For the fruit bar therein, one would kill.

If you ever wanted to see greed gleam out of the observer's eye, watch the guy who didn't find a fruit bar in his K-ration.

These were the caviar of the foxholes, the nectar from the Gods.

Whether it was intended or not, the little packs of four cigarettes found in the K-rations guaranteed the addiction that has made millionaires out of lung surgeons.

It is called "lead in" advertising.

ELEANOR

One very dark night, we received a radio call to pick up two wounded.

Whitmore very carefully eased the jeep up as closely to the battle area as possible and we took off overland.

When we arrived at Company C, we found that there was one more casualty than expected, so Sgt. Adams sent me back to the jeep for another litter.

Well, I am really moderately night blind, so I was stumbling all over the place. What I didn't know was that the enemy position was a salient point, in other words cutting into our lines like a knife, and when I heard German conversation, I realized I was in enemy territory.

"Ver ist das?"

"Hans!", I answered.

"Ver ist das?"

"Erich!"

"Ver geht's?"

"Gottfried!"

Pretty soon, I was running out of German names.

Then, I heard the Heavenly sounds of "Fuck" and "Shit" and I knew I was getting near American positions again.

Then, I went into a cold sweat. How was I going to get over to the other side without getting shot by my own guys?

I dropped to my hands and knees and started crawling. I was whispering as loudly as I dared: "Don't shoot, I'm American! Don't shoot, I'm American" until I was nose to muzzle with an M1 rifle.

"I'll blow your fuckin' brains out if you move another inch!" It was so good to hear the mother tongue, again!

He was in a nice deep foxhole with some others, that I was just dying to crawl into.

I got the usual question given to suspected spies or infiltrators: "Who won the World Series?" "Who was Babe Ruth?" and all that crap, which almost got me shot, because of my un-American disinterest in the Holy Game."

Finally, the non-com in charge asked me: "What do you think of Eleanor Roosevelt?"

"Are you a Democrat or a Republican?" I asked.

"What the hell difference does that make?"

"Are you a Democrat or a Republican?"

"I'm a Republican!"

"OK! Eleanor Roosevelt is a whore, and Franklin Roosevelt is a fucking socialist dictator!"

"Let him come in, Ernie, he's O. K.!"

DAS BOOT

By late February, I was coming down with the "Immortality Syndrome."

Lawson and I had developed a macabre fraternity house type of humor, which psychologists might interpret as a defensive mechanism against the horrors we were witnessing.

We began a series of adventures that drove Sgt. Adams up the walls.

Probably, the most insane was the afternoon we were called about one kilometer up the bank of a stream to pick up several American and German casualties.

There was no way of getting our jeep down the narrow foot path along the bank, so the prospect was we would have to hand-carry these men a long way.

"I wish we had a boat to float them down," said Detroit.

"Great idea!" I answered.

Lawson looked at me with narrowing eyes: "What do you have in mind?"

I pointed across the stream: "Let's see if someone has a boat in that little village over there."

We walked to the old stone bridge that the Germans had blown up in retreat.

Detroit rebelled: "You guys are nuts! I'm not going over there!" He turned and went back to the others.

Lawson and I crawled and jumped from stone to stone until we reached the other bank.

As we walked into the village, my blood ran cold. One could always rely on our intelligence boys! They had told us all of the Germans had pulled out of this area.

There was a German squad in the street, led by some kind of junior officer. They were looking very Hollywood movie-like as their jaws dropped and they gawked at us.

I grabbed Lawson's arm: "Don't run!"

Then, I shifted into "Chicago casual" and walked up with confident torso and shaking knees to the officer, a handsome black-haired Teutonic. His troops had us covered with their Mausers.

We had three things going for us:

First, I spoke German well enough so that they might believe I was a German-American.

Second, Germans generally react positively to arrogance, with which I was amply endowed.

Third, and probably the real reason we got away with it was that German medics were not in the army. They were civilians, like our Red Cross.

I didn't ask for a boat for our wounded. I demanded one!

The young officer told me in precise German where I and our wounded could go.

"And, how about your wounded?"

"Our wounded?"

"Yes. They are in even worse shape than ours!" Which was the truth.

I think at that point the officer just wanted to get rid of us and not be burdened with prisoners. "Get them a boat," he snapped to a couple of villagers.

We scurried off after them toward the stream, wondering whether we were going to get some Mauser bullets in our backs.

"Why the hell do I ever listen to you?" Lawson was muttering under his breath.

Then we discovered where all the river boats had gone. The local villagers had sunk them in the stream, held down by heavy rocks. They jumped into the water up to their shoulders and began removing the rocks from one. Suddenly, it popped up like a cork.

They were tipping the boat to drain it, when I heard this roar from across the stream: "Whitey!"

There, looking like an African Safari team stretched out along the bank were Adams and the other boys with casualties slung between them.

"Get over here!"

"Wait until we drain the boat!"

"Now!"

I became sarcastic: "Do you want us to swim across?"

"No, walk! That should be no problem for you!"

He was mad.

He walked on refusing to look or talk to us again. Meanwhile, we were getting facial: "Nah-nahs" from the good boys who had stayed with teacher, especially Detroit.

We pushed the villagers away and jumped into the ankle deep water in the boat and started floating and rowing parallel to the others.

"Wanna use the boat, Sergeant?"

He continued to ignore us.

I was beginning to feel very guilty about us floating easily on the stream while the others were sweating and straining on the bank.

We whined: "Can we come over, now?"

Still no answer.

We rowed furiously down stream and pulled up to the opposite bank. Crawling out, of course, we sank waist deep into the marsh, and by the time we made it up the bank, we were slimy with mud.

The safari bore down upon us, and we stepped aside until Adams was abreast. He was uncompromising! "Take the last litter," he barked.

If you think that carrying a 180 pound man 3 kilometers on your slimy shoulders with slimy hands isn't punishment enough, join the Marines!

THE DAY ROOSEVELT DIED

Certainly, the saddest day of my combat career was April 12, 1945.

The morning started badly. We had packed our gear the night before in preparation for moving into this new town.

When we arrived at the new location bird-dogged by Lt. Herman, Captain Coburn, commander of C company was standing in the room, looking off into nowhere with a "Sgt. Wagner look" on his face.

It seems that his company had been ambushed when it was coming in to clear the town the night before and twenty-four of his men were dead in a ditch about fifty yards out back of our new aid station.

I had the feeling that we had another Captain Daley evacuation to tag.

Daley had been the commander of Company A since its inception two years before. Every one of his original men had become like family to him.

That fact bothered his aidman, Marovich. "He's too close to these guys. He's going to crack up if he loses any of them."

Marovich was right. Daley's company was one of the first to get into combat and after the second time, the "battle of the quarry," we got a call from Marovich to come pick-up Capt. Daley.

There he sat, completely stressed out, with a destination tag pinned onto his jacket. He had that blank "Sgt. Wagner" look on his face.

I led this dignified, kind-hearted gentleman and superb officer by the hand to the jeep, where I sat him gently in the front seat.

Some of his men were milling around with tears in their eyes.

One, bent over and said: "Goodbye, Captain," and then collapsed onto his shoulder, crying.

Captain Daley responded to nothing. Head erect, he was staring blankly into the distance.

I couldn't take any more of this. I jumped into the back of the jeep and Whitmore took off.

I hadn't really know Captain Daley, so I recovered emotionally quickly. But, Captain Coburn was another matter. I knew him well and we could even be called friends. My emotions nose dived precipitously.

When I passed in front of him, recognition spread on his face. "Whitey!" He grasped my arm. Then, after a moment: "Do you want to see my boys?"

That was the last thing I wanted to do but I politely followed him out the back door into the field.

There, in this long drainage ditch, spaced irregularly in various frozen postures, was the cream of his Company.

Some were replacement riflemen that he hardly knew, but he stopped at those who were from the original group telling me their names and something about them.

Lt. Herman came out to get us. The graves registration guys were on the way and he wanted to evacuate Captain Coburn before the body pickup began.

Some local farmers were pressed into service to bring the bodies out of the field.

I went upstairs and watched as they stacked the bodies German-style, neatly, like cord wood, all heads in the same direction in a wooden farm wagon in the yard across the street.

Then, graves registration arrived, got up onto the wagon and dumped these one by one, helter-skelter, on top of one another in two jeep-drawn carriers. Even the German villagers seemed shocked.

In this theater of the absurd, the last body was dropped in the corner of the carrier with an arm on either edge. It looked as if he were simply sunbathing.

I wondered, even as case-hardened as I had become, how the loved ones in the states of these no longer useful bodies would feel about this casual treatment, if they knew about it.

I looked out the side window, and there was Lt. Herman, newly washed and uniformed, with his aviator scarf tucked into his shirt, leaning against a tree, blissfully unaffected by the tragedy about him, writing home to family. You see, he was still alive.

Things couldn't get worse, I thought.

But, they could.

When I went downstairs, Detroit had his ear into our radio.

"President Roosevelt died!"

I couldn't believe it! God doesn't die! That's what he had been, our secular God. He was the man who saved America! Our leader! One of the greats of our Century! Dead?

And, Harry Truman president?

I walked into our sleeping quarters. Missouri, Fitzpatrick, Walsh and Watters were already playing pinochle.

"Franklin Roosevelt is dead!" I said simply.

The guys looked at me, and shared my amazement and dismay.

I thought.

Missouri brightened: "You're from Chicago, Whitey. How do you think the Cubs will do this year?"

Later in the afternoon, I heard some yelling out back.

I went to the window. The boy's from Coburn's Company were out beyond the drainage ditches from which their buddies had so recently been removed and were involved in a pickup game of softball.

Life does go on, doesn't it?

I went out and joined them.

PANZERFAUST

I would like to dedicate this to those who, like John Wayne, glorify combat without ever knowing what it is to soil one's underpants in action.

I started out taking a simple tourist photo and became involved in a horror.

We were having a short R&R break in this little town.

We had all washed up and were looking pretty spiffy.

The tank guys had opened up their hatches and were airing out and cleaning up the interiors.

I still have the photo that Lawson took of me standing in front of this one tank.

We walked over to the side of the tank and were trying to reload this strange camera we had "liberated", when a German lady in her late sixties, the type of "Frau" you could use as a stereotype advertisement for "Gemutlichkeit," stepped out from behind her front fence three houses down with what looked like a broom.

This hardly drew my attention because I was accustomed to seeing such ladies come out to sweep the streets every day.

I froze when she pointed this thing in our direction and I realized it was a panzerfaust, an explosive dish that was propelled off the stick like a rocket.

To this day, I still see it in slow motion:

This lady with the neatly tied back hair, flowered dress and neat white apron, fired. The explosive must have ricochet on the open lid of the driver's side and there was this muffled explosion inside. If the thing had hit the outside of the tank, this story would not have been written.

Instantly, ammunition began exploding inside the tank.

The tanker who was sitting with his legs inside the turret fell backward with mangled legs off of the tank on one side while the other standing next to him fell off on our side.

Lawson and I were deafened and stunned.

Then, a terrible racket ensued. Every rifleman who had a weapon let loose at this lady. The machine guns on the other two tanks were swiveled around and tracer bullets were slashing down the street.

The non-coms were screaming for everyone to stop -- it was too dangerous for others. But months of death and hell were all being taken out on that one little old lady who undoubtedly saw herself only as a defender of her fatherland.

Lawson told me later that he did not believe there was enough left of her to bury.

I didn't see, because the next thing I heard was a scream.

One of the medics from the 2nd battalion had reached in to pull out one of the two men inside. He pulled him up to the waist, then screamed: "Where is the rest of him?" He let go of the hand and stood up totally blanched.

Fitzpatrick was fantastic in crises. He jumped through the turret and soon was dragging the other tanker out under the armpits: "Get the jeep," he was shouting.

Our aide station was still two kilometers back at the last town.

The tanker with the bad legs was put in the front seat of the jeep next to Fitzpatrick. The other with a broken arm and the man from the interior of the tank were placed on the litters mounted on back.

We had no safety straps, nor time to find any, so I got between the two men on the litters, wrapped my legs around the one with the broken arm and my arms around the other, and Fitzpatrick took off at mach one.

When I looked more closely the man's face, I realized in what bad shape he was. Bones were sticking through his jaw, as if he had suffered an explosion inside of his body. I really thought he was dead.

When we got on the road, Fitzpatrick went tearing at an unbelievable speed and we were bouncing in and out of shell hole remainders from the previous day's engagement.

When we were about one kilometer out of town, we discovered that there was still enemy in the woods on either side of the road. A string of German mortars were tracking us with shells.

Fitzpatrick was incredible! He kept control of the jeep, even though we were up in the air twenty-five percent of the time.

All the bouncing and noise revived the tanker whom I was holding and he went berserk, lashing out, trying to rise and get away, with only my arms keeping him from falling off.

He began beating on my body, my face, everywhere.

The man on the other litter was trying to help me with his one good arm.

Incredibly, the man with the mangled legs got up on his knees in the front set and tried to hold the tanker's swinging arms.

By the time we had reached the aid station, I was a battered mess.

I sat on the jeep outside while the boys inside were working on the casualties. Detroit was treating my wounds. Aside from the body, I had bruises on my cheeks, a black eye, and a bloody nose. "Can you get a purple heart when the wounds inflicted are from your own side," he joked.

Fitzpatrick came out of the aid station: "You got beaten up for nothing. He died on the table."

On the way back, I was thinking about the strange fate that had interfaced these dead and injured boys from America with this non-combatant German woman.

Lawson took one look at my face and said: "We were lucky we took that picture before this happened!"

KAMIKAZE

Let me tell you about the first time I began thinking of "fragging" Captain Wilson.

We had finally reached the Siegfried Line, that so-called impregnable fortress line of defense set up the length of the French-German border in the late 1930s.

There is no question that the Allies considered this the ultimate battle, with potentially huge losses.

Our assault was two days away, and our Division needed to know how strong the German defenses were in front of the line.

It was decided to send a squad of riflemen in the early morning hours of the next day to report by radio at dawn.

The problem was, in returning in the early morning daylight, the squad was within range of one nest of German machine guns at one point and another nest beyond that.

In other words, it was : "You are on your own, guys! Get to hell out of there as best you can."

In light of this, the morale of this reconnaissance squad was very low, so they asked for medics to go along.

A staff officer went to Captain Wilson, who approved the idea without the slightest humane considerations regarding its lethal nature and assigned our squad. Of course, he did not want to lose Missouri or Watters, so he substituted Dutch and Detroit to join Lawson and me.

It mattered not to him that our instructions were to drop the litters and run and that there was absolutely no useful purpose for our being there except to give a morale boost to what was in effect a suicide mission. Why worry? He had a pool of replacements available at Regiment to fill his future needs.

Sgt. Adams was beside himself. He pleaded with the Captain, who looked at him with that bland, frozen, now hateful expression until Adams gave up.

Our group retired to our sleeping bags.

I wrote a farewell letter, similar to the one I had read in that German diary on New Year's Day and gave it to Adams to mail if the worst happened.

We were very morose. It was one thing to die attempting to save people. It was another to perish on a useless mission.

At about midnight, I heard the jeep pull up. I looked out the window. It was Lt. Herman returning from H.Q.

Adams walked out and was talking to him. Herman seemed very agitated. He jumped out of the jeep and came into our room. He looked at us for a moment, then went into the aid station.

We heard loud voices and then shouting. It was the Captain and Lt. Herman. Herman slammed out of the station, into the jeep and drove off into the night.

I fell into a fitful sleep.

At about 3:00 AM, Adams came to wake us up. We thought it was to go. He looked very calm. "Lt. Herman got the whole mission called off. Go back to sleep."

And sleep I did, like no other time again in my life.

Lt. Herman had exercised his pull with his relative at the H.Q. and talked them into using air reconnaissance.

I knew, what Lt. Herman was too decent to suspect, that Captain Wilson was in a rage at his being overruled by a subordinate. I could just see him searching the files in his beady brain trying to find a way to get rid of Herman.

That's when the thought of "fragging" Wilson slipped into my mind.

THE DAY I CAPTURED GERMANY

The assault upon the Siegfried Line still seems like a fantasy.

Out of the pure accident of rotation, our division was assigned to make the approach, our regiment was to spearhead the penetration, and our battalion was to make the break through.

Then, our companies were to leap-frog each other until Company A, to which I was attached, became the ultimate point of the entire Seventh Army effort.

It was very heady and very dangerous.

I had already learned that the best place to be on an approach is at the very point because the enemy tries to get as many casualties as possible by lobbing shells into the center of a column.

Therefore, for a short time, I would be the very point man of the entire Allied effort to conquer Germany.

As a matter of fact, like many other developments in warfare, the anticipated dangerous turns out to be pussycat and the unexpected develops into horror.

But, I leap ahead of my story.

At 2:00 AM, every damn piece of heavy artillery in the entire Seventh army was massed behind our division and went off like a colossal Fourth of July event, pounding the hell out of the pillboxes beyond the forward tank barriers of the Siegfried line.

At 4:00 AM, the "artificial moonlight" went on. That is the reflection of every spotlight in the Seventh Army against the clouds to permit us vision to move up to the tank barriers.

By dawn, we were ready to break through. The engineers had run a "mine clearing" to the right of the main road barriers so that the riflemen and the tanks could go around them.

When the order to move out came, my pervasive memory is of our "fearless leader" Missouri hiding on the safe side of one concrete tank barrier, with Walker shrinking behind him, pointing around the barrier for us to charge. I swore he would never be my "leader" again.

As we advanced down the road toward the defensive heights about a half a mile away, riflemen were peeling off to the left and the right to drop explosive charges through the slots in the nearby concrete pillboxes. We could not understand why we were not receiving defensive fire.

We continued the company leap-frogging until Sgt. Riley and I were, indeed, the point men into the Fatherland.

The quiet was eerie. All we could hear were the tanks rolling behind us and a staccato of pillbox purifications.

Riley shot to me out of the side of his mouth: "They're waiting up there! They're waiting up there! We are sitting ducks! This is an ambush!"

I couldn't disagree with him. If he was right, this was the worst place in the entire U.S. Army to be at that time.

As the long khaki line wended closer to the heights, my ears were ringing, I was drenched with sweat and expecting to be impacted with machine gun bullets at any moment.

At about a city block's distance from the heights, we couldn't take it anymore.

"Let's die fighting!"

The whole company broke ranks and took off across the field whooping like a civil war charge and clambered up the heights.

"Empty!"

"Nobody here!"

"They took off during the night!"

We were taking no chances. We jumped into the elaborate network of trenches on the plateau and the guys started setting up defenses.

The tanks came rumbling up the side road and joined us. The officers gathered. All were bewildered. No one knew what to do. We were expecting the worst battle since Normandy and we had:

NOTHING!

We were paradoxically in a state of letdown. It was like an aborted orgasm!

About noon, the word came that the Germans were in full retreat and we got orders to move over the mountain to the first town in Germany. Adams told me to wait by the side of the road for Lt. Herman to return from the

H.Q. and to tell him what had happened.

It took almost half-an-hour for the entire column to disappear over the ridge, and for another half-hour I was alone in the deathly still of Hitler's greatest defensive structure.

Lt. Herman and Whitmore came streaking up the road.

"Gone an hour, eh?" Herman pulled out his inevitable map case. "There's this little road going down along the side of the mountain. Maybe, we can head them off at the pass!"

Ever the romantic, like General Patton, he stood up and pointed to the right and almost fell out when Whitmore made a fast turn.

In short time, we reached the next town. It was obvious the Germans were giving up. They were milling around all over the place, some 10,000 of them, all trying to dump their rifles into, and surrender to our medical jeep.

I got a Nazi flag, a dagger, a Luger, field glasses, a Leica..........

Then, Whitmore asked the Lieutenant, "Have you seen any other American troops, yet?"

"No! Have you, Whitey?"

"No!!"

Whitmore turned the wheel sharply and headed us to hell out of town! We went straight up the main road back toward the Siegfried Line.

About one kilometer up, we met the division column coming over the mountain. A whole line of tanks and troops stretching over the horizon with division second in command in the front jeep. The anti-mine personnel were diligently panning their mine sweepers back and forth over the road in front of him.

All looked up frozen in astonishment.

Whitmore swung us up to the side of the command jeep. There we sat, three unarmed medics with red crosses on our helmets.

Herman: "Go ahead in, General! We've already secured the town for you!"

RETRIBUTION

After the Siegfried Line, at every free moment, I was consumed with the problem of how to kill Captain Wilson. I was dedicated to that proposition.

I fantasized all sorts of scenarios.

Then the opportunity presented itself.

We were set up for a few days in an aid station on a road bordering a river. At first we believed the other side of the river to be free of the enemy, but Dutch disabused us of that comfort on the first evening when he came rushing in with his pants at half-hitch. He had been using the slit trench we dug about 20 feet out from the building when tracer bullets began to stream past him.

We were under sporadic sniper fire.

Later that night, Wilson handed me a still booted lower leg he had been forced to amputate and told me to bury it in the back.

I found a spot far out and in the dark was digging a hole with my entrenching tool, when I hit some metal. My heart stopped. I thought I had hit a mine.

I felt around it, and realized it was a rifle left when the Germans moved out.

The plan fell into place: If this rifle is loaded.....we are under sniper fire.....Wilson has to come out to use the slit trench.....

I quickly shoveled some leafs and branches over the rifle, buried the leg, and went back into the aid station.

All night in my sleeping bag I was reviewing my plan.

The next morning I was able to slip out and check the rifle. It was loaded. I reburied it.

That night, I was the only one covering the aid station with Captain Wilson in the back reading. I was shaking with nervousness.

I heard a vehicle pull up in the dark. It was Lerner in his ambulance with a rifleman who had stepped on a shoe box mine.

I called Capt. Wilson out and helped Lerner carry the poor guy in. He was in shock. We put him on the table and Lerner took off.

There was just Wilson, the rifleman and myself under the single bright Coleman lantern.

Wilson cocked his head and looked at the leg. Then, he picked it up at the knee and the muscle and meat fell away from the shin bone and was swinging from the bottom of the knee. The entire shin bone was bared.

I was trying not to throw up and Wilson looked at me very sharply. I held back. "Get the plasma going!" he said.

I rolled the rack over to the table and was having a hell of a time finding a decent vein.

He took a sterile gauze pad, held the end of the shin bone with it and then said: "Hold this!" My stomach was churning again, but I took it.

My brain was screaming: "Amputate! Amputate! Get it over with!"

Wilson stood back, examining the lower leg through his wire frame glasses and rubbing his chin slowly.

"I think we can save this."

"You're crazy!" I thought.

Any other aid station would have given primary care, then wrapped the leg and sent the boy back to the field hospital for amputation. But, not Wilson.

He starting humming, loosened the tourniquet on the upper leg to let some blood flow, and then went over and poured a mess of hot water from the top of the stove into a large pan. He cooled it with some other water and I think he added some disinfectant.

My arm was really beginning to cramp from holding the weight of that leg, so I switched to the other hand and eventually was bracing with both hands.

Wilson was in his own world, humming away like a craftsman in his shop. I think he forgot I was there.

Then he came over, removed the boot carefully and put the pan under the dangling tissue.

I was fighting waves of nausea, but I would not break down in front of this man!

"Dip," he said, and I lowered the shin bone. The tissue became partially submerged. He had a small brush and was humming as he was scrubbing away, scrubbing away, getting every piece of mud and debris out of the fibers. Then, he walked away, emptied the bucket and repeated the process again. "I think we have it now!"

He dumped sulfa into the length of the cavity, slowly eased the bone back down and lined up the ankle bones, humming all the time.

As he began the stitching job, I was looking at his face.

Just Wilson, the rifleman and me under the single Coleman lantern.

How could this man who repaired damaged bodies so superbly, be so unconscious of the spirits they contained. How could he be so sensitive and responsive to physical wounds and so insensitive and unresponsive to psychic needs?

"I am not doing a final stitch on this, they'll have to open it again to avoid infection." I am not sure he was really speaking to me.

He did a superb bandaging job, stood back and looked at it, then started off toward the back room flipped over his shoulder: "Get an ambulance, and get him down to field." And, he was off. He was done. He probably forgot the man as he was leaving the room to go back to his book.

I stood in awe of this man's talent.

How often in later life I would meet men and women like him, superb and humane in their chosen fields and inhumane in their personal relationships. Musicians, artists, teachers, medical men....people from all fields. I still don't understand it. I've simply learned to live with it.

The next day, I buried the gun next to the amputated leg.

EASTER IN HEIDELBERG

I am repeatedly impressed by the role that pure chance plays in human events.

As everyone knows now, Heidelberg, having no industrial or strategic importance, remained standing to become one of the most important towns in Germany after V.E. Day.

But, how it escaped damage on the day it was captured is not generally known.

In fact, I didn't really know, myself, until I read about it in the Saturday Evening Post in 1948.

It was 3:00 AM on Easter morning of 1945, and our column was moving in the bright moonlight on a road bordering the Neckar River toward Heidelberg.

We passed what was left of the ancient city of Mannheim, empty shells and empty windows through which the moonlight hopscotched. A sad end for a city that had hosted such musical greats as Mozart and Spohr.

The light of dawn was just showing as we approached the out skirts of Heidelberg.

A shot rang out!

The jeeps, tanks and other vehicles did sharp U-turns to retrace our route to better defensive positions.

Captain Coburn was calling back for artillery, when he was told that the city had just surrendered and the German troops were already pulling out.

The officers didn't really trust this, so we made a "battle ready" advance into the town. Some of the guys were walking on their elbows to look cautiously around buildings, when at 6:00 AM all the church bells in town went off. It was time for Easter Services.

The Burghers and their families emerged en masse out of their homes as if a major invasion were not taking place.

They were stepping over prone riflemen, saying "Enchuldige mich!" and moving on to the churches.

For years, that morning puzzled me.

Why had the German troops withdrawn at that late hour?

The Saturday Evening Post article answered this.

A Colonel in the U. S. Army had been a classmate of the man who was then mayor of Heidelberg.

In the early morning hours, he had been able to get the Mayor on the phone and arrange to save this treasured city. The Mayor persuaded the German officers to leave.

The shot?

That was a disgruntled old man, who shot an old musket at the infernal invaders.

Upon such improbable coincidences are the fates of cities and States determined.

WHOSE OX IS GORED?

We overestimated how far the German army had withdrawn from Heidelberg. As a matter of fact, they had stopped at Neckargemund, the next town a few kilometers down the Neckar River.

By the time I got there, the fighting had ended and the fun had begun.

The boys had "liberated" a trainload of the finest French Champagne routed for the elite in Berlin. They were passing it out at the roadside, a case to each vehicle and a bottle to each rifleman.

Within an hour, if the Germans had counter-attacked, they could have wiped out the cream of our regiment, who would have died happy, however.

Can you imagine city and country boys guzzling down a drink that tastes like soda water?

Even I, sophisticate that I was, conked out on the aid station operating table.

It was a heady day, indeed!

When I revived, I popped some aspirins and went outside.

Someone had bird-dogged the local whore house which was directly across from our station, and the line was already half way down the block.

Most of our guys were out in front gathered around the jeep. Detroit and I walked over to an archway about a block away and commenced photographing each other.

There was a dead German soldier lying face up about 10 paces from us being looked at very nervously by a line of German civilians waiting to get into a shop across the street.

An American jeep roared in to pick him up.

Being as high on champagne as the rest of us and seeing the civilians in the bleachers, the guys decided to be really gross. They picked the body up by the head and the feet, swung him back and forth a couple of times and then heaved him into the back seat like sack of potatoes.

There was civilian hysteria: screaming, vomiting and fainting.

To tell you the truth, the champagne wasn't setting too well in my stomach either.

The guys just hopped into the jeep and nonchalantly drove off.

Every time I see a picture of a death camp corpse being thrown into an oven, that scene at Neckargemund comes back to me.

I reflect upon the reaction of the Germans to the mistreatment of their own and remember the old saying: "It depends upon whose ox is gored."

THE RIPPLE EFFECT OF THE BULLET

After the Neckargemund incident, I found that I had hardened to the point where I could sit on the edge of our jeep munching a K-ration while I stared at another German corpse lying face up in the road.

He was the usual straight haired blonde, hints of ruddy complexion not yet faded from his face, looking up into nowhere.

I wonder how far the damage of that American bullet had rippled. Besides stopping his, what other lives had it altered forever?

Like his countrymen who reacted at the arch in Neckargemund, pain has this ripple effect.

Is there a wife?

Is there a child?

Certainly, there must have been parents.

How about friends and relatives, schoolmates, fellow workers, and neighbors?

Was this guy a nationalistic Nazi, or, like most of us, drawn into a war he didn't want, either.

I felt a strange communion of spirits.

We were really in the same boat.

It was just a matter of who got it first.

THE LAIR OF THE SS

There are defining events in some lives where one ceases only being acted upon, and becomes a principal actor one's self.

Such an event for me occurred on a mountain top in the Black Forest, when we blundered into the hideout of what was left of (what I have been told later was) the most feared of the Hitler's SS, the 17th Waffen SS Division.

At this point in the war, there was a vast difference between battling a demoralized regular German army composed mostly of teenagers and aging men, and the SS, young, healthy and dedicated.

I say blundered, because at this point in April of 1945, the Wehrmacht was strategically retreating to permit the Western Allies to conquer as much of Germany as possible before the Russians arrived. So we believed we were primarily engaged in a routine sweeping and clearing operation.

One morning we were dropped off of the trucks on a mountain road with one day's supply of provisions, to sweep through a mountainous area and be picked up on a road on the other side.

It wasn't until late afternoon when we reached the top of the highest of the mountains that the fire-fight broke out.

I went prone next to an officer I had never met before, Lt. Anderson, new commander of B Company.

He smiled and said: "This is what the manual calls being pinned down by enemy fire." I liked him instantly!

We did not yet know these were SS we had encountered.

We dug in for in for the evening, expecting the opponent to retreat by morning.

We were awakened about 2:00 AM by the roar of small arms fire and German voices yelling "Whatevers" in the night.

I lay face up watching tracer bullets slicing ever closer through the rampart behind my head. I dared not move an inch.

Finally, the firing subsided, and all we could hear were the cries of the wounded and dying.

By morning, the SS had withdrawn to where we were able to get out of our holes and assess the damage.

We had some dead and wounded from both sides. A German medical detail of four had also been captured.

The dead were hauled into the shrubbery, and the wounded and the German medics were concentrated in the center of the circle of foxholes.

The SS had dug in around our perimeter. They had nowhere else to go.

We had a real problem. We had started with only one day's supply of food and water, no second tier medical equipment, such as plasma and lots of wounded. We were in trouble!

The medics had to set up something, but our fearless leader Corporal Missouri, was cowering as usual in our foxhole, tightly embraced by Watters whose only sin was not evil intent, but low intelligence.

I was sure Missouri was weaving up some fanciful tales of heroism with which to later entertain Captain Wilson.

I had enough of Missouri's screwing up our work.

I got out of the fox hole and attempted to set up some rational medical protocol. Lawson was very upset that I was superseding Missouri's authority, but I was fed up with submitting myself to the dangers created by this coward's self-protective conduct.

Some of the American boys had lost a lot of blood, and there was one I did not expect to live. He was a hardy guy from North Carolina, who had a bullet hole that I could look into right between his eyes, as well as a bullet in his forearm. Lord knows where the bullet in the head had come to rest.

Lawson splinted his arm, while I cut down a bandage that still ended up covering his eyes.

Meanwhile, sniper bullets were still impacting the trees around us and ricochetting all over the place.

With the other wounded, we could do no more than apply our large bandages and inject morphine. I felt totally helpless.

Lt. Anderson was looking down into the foxhole at us.

"Anything, I can do?"

"Yeah! Cook me up some plasma!"

"Why don't you call down for some on my radio?"

He led me to his makeshift command post and his radio man got our headquarters on the band. I asked for sulfa, bandages, morphine, plasma and some surgical tools.

It turned out to be in vain, as the helicopter drops were swept away from us by the wind patterns at the top of the mountain.

PERFECT FRIENDSHIP

Lt. Anderson and I developed one of those instant friendships. He was one of those well-bred, athletic people that I admired. We lounged about the rest of the day discussing the North Shore of Chicago and his college, Northwestern, that I now hoped to attend. I had the feeling, if we both survived the war, we could be lifelong friends.

We entered into the second night feeling very dismal. Sniper fire was constant. Our meager food supply was almost exhausted and our canteens were almost empty.

Meanwhile, the German medics, without any rations at all, had hunkered down with their wounded in a foxhole nearby.

We were very worried about another night attack, but it didn't come.

Then, one of those unexpected pivotal events:

During the night, the German wounded, having no supply of water at all, were keeping us up crying repeatedly and in pain, "Vasser....Vasser".

"Fuck, 'em," said one rifleman.

"Shoot them, before they drive us crazy," said another.

At 2:00 AM, I couldn't take it anymore. I walked over to their foxhole, where the German medics, thinking perhaps that we were going to shoot them, were looking very pale in the moonlight.

I am a very light water drinker, so I still had half of a canteen left. I gave it to the medics for their wounded.

When I returned, I got some pretty rough handling by the rifleman.

"You waste our good water on those bastards!"

The miracle began the next morning.

First thing, the German medics came over to tend our wounded. They were far better trained than we were.

They went into the foxholes and laid down boughs of branches and shrubs to get our wounded off of the bare ground.

They showed us how to arrange coats and our few blankets to give them better wind protection and administered some of their own drugs, which we were previously unable to appropriate because we could not interpret the labels.

In short, we saved everybody, including the North Carolinian, who had removed his head bandage and was walking around with the hole in his forehead helping the German medics.

I was constantly amazed at the survival stamina of these mountain boys.

The next morning, Lt. Anderson called me over for a Pow-wow with the other company officers.

They had been advised that Regiment was planning a breakthrough to relieve us, and the question of whether our battalion, outnumbered by a whole regiment of SS, should simultaneously launch a pincer type breakout was the subject.

I was called in because of the problem of the wounded.

I was completely accepted by the officers.

It must have looked strange, two Captains, two first Lieutenants and one skinny medical private with a Red Cross on his helmet in a strategy conference.

The officers broke up the meeting to wait for further instructions from the Regiment.

I did not know at that time that Lt. Herman, Sgt. Adams and Whitmore, attempting to bring us medical supplies in the jeep, had been ambushed on the road that morning and taken captive.

As Ye Sow...

Tragedy struck!

At about noon, I heard a shot ring out!

I paid no more attention to that than any other sniper shots we endured during the day, until Sgt. Riley of Anderson's company scurried over: "Anderson's been hit!"

I rushed back with him. There, on the lumber road adjoining our site, lay Anderson, with canteens strewn all about him.

He had been playing the unselfish hero role for his boys, ignoring the risk. He crossed the sniper-covered road to go to the stream below with a bunch of canteens and got hit coming back.

I almost violated my own rule by leaping forward to get to Anderson. Sgt. Riley was holding me back: "They've got the road covered!"

Anderson pulled his now inappropriate joke from the road: "This is what the manual calls `being pinned down by hostile fire!'"

We were pacing back and forth trying to figure out how to get him off the road without further casualties, when I felt a hand upon my shoulder. It was one of the German medics with the others behind him, carrying one of our litters. He pushed us back, and all four of them went onto the road and gently lifted and brought Anderson back to safety. They knew the Germans would not shoot their own medics.

How a little kindness pays off!

They set him up with some comfort near his command post, and I commenced watching my new friend slowly die.

Anderson had been hit at the point where his right leg joined his body, so the wound did not look serious, but when the Germans probed for the bullet and couldn't find it they looked very glum. They assumed correctly that the bullet had ricochetted off the pelvic bone and done great mischief on its trajectory upward.

They shook their heads and left.

I sat there, while his men straggled by in small groups to cheer him up. Obvious concern etched their faces.

At first, he was his convivial self as we discussed home and college again but after an hour, he had faded into white oblivion.

I sat there looking like Sgt. Wagner at his worst.

After about half-an-hour, Captain Coburn wrapped his arm about me and said: "We've got to get him out of sight. His men are really upset."

Lawson and Watters took the ends of the litter, and I followed them to some distant shrubbery, where they did what we had learned to do at the railroad tracks. They tipped the litter over and dumped him into the bushes. He was longer useful to the war effort. "Litters and aid men are for the living!"

He looked so vulnerable there, face down, with his pants down to his knees. I made Watters help me pull them back up. "At least, let him lie there in dignity!"

"Good bye, good friend, short as it was!"

A TALE OF TWO WORLDS

Why had the death of Anderson affected me so much more than any other loss I had witnessed?

I believe it was because with Anderson, I had stepped over that invisible psychological social line that separates societies. He had accepted me as a social equal in the artificially structured institution called the U. S. Army, and from that time forward I refused to accept the psychological demeaning that is the weapon of the privileged.

Since he had accepted me as a leader, the other officers had accepted me also, and I would never be able to return to the Army's underclass mentality again.

I did not have too much time to brood because that night word got to me that a young German had crawled into our positions and surrendered. Since, he was wounded, he had been turned over the German medics.

I went over to their foxholes and sure enough, there was this young man in a Luftwaffe uniform, his thigh being bandaged by their medics.

He spoke perfect English. Our boys, who were gathered around him, were totally charmed. I sat there and listened for a while and discovered that he had, indeed, been a pilot and when the Luftwaffe was shot into extinction, like our ASTP boys, he had been dropped into the infantry, in this case the SS. He was wounded in the fire fight of the first night.

He claimed he hated the group and crawled away as soon as he was able.

I was inclined to believe him. He was obviously from an aristocratic family, and his contempt for Hitler and the Nazis seemed genuine. In short, he charmed the hell out of me also.

The longer we talked, the warmer the relationship. This son of aristocracy from Germany and this son of middle class immigrants to America had far more that bonded them than separated them, and yet because of the immutable forces of history, we were assigned to be deadly enemies.

These two nineteen-year-olds talked deep into the night about those things that should occupy the minds of nineteen-year-olds -- and not about the blunders of the elders that had cast them into the horror of mutual annihilation.

You Can't Go Home Again

By the next morning the SS had pulled out, obviously learning that there was relief in strength massing. We started to move everything and everybody towards our original rendezvous road, when a rifleman called Sgt. Riley over.

There on the path lay a dead American soldier.

"Who is he?" None of the officers or non-coms knew.

They pulled out his dog tags and Riley looked at his roster: "Oh! My God! He was that replacement that joined us on the road when we were starting out!" He had never met or spoken to any other member of the platoon.

He was the platoon's "unknown soldier."

No war could not have been shorter for a rifleman.

When we returned to the aid station, our mail was waiting. My mother had sent to her starving son macaroons and cans of anchovies, "Something the Army doesn't serve!" she wrote.

To this day, I hate anchovies.

Missouri had preceded us, already regaling Captain Wilson with his "heroics," and slipping to him privately how I had usurped his authority.

I certainly would not expect Watters to support me, and Lawson was showing the true colors that served him so well later in his corporate rise: Abandon friends and play the winning side.

Sgt. Adams, who recognized Missouri's true colors, was no longer with us, nor Lt. Herman, who might have intervened for me.

I had returned, recognized as an equal abroad, but still subordinated at home. I felt pretty much alone.

What really incinerated Wilson, however, was when Grossman, one of the company aid men, came in to advise him that the line officers recommended that Wilson put me in for a Silver Star.

"All that son of a bitch did was talk more than anyone else, disobey his corporal and get my MAC, First Sergeant and Jeep driver captured!" Grossman reported this to me.

The reality was, as far as losing Lt. Herman for him, Wilson owed me a Silver Star for that alone.

There was no question about it, anymore. I was going to be assigned to a combat platoon.

LETTERS TO MOTHER AND OTHER LIES

After my mother passed away, we found a box in which she had saved every scrap I had written during this period, which, me being one of the Army's champion "letters to mother" writers, was considerable.

When I laid these out chronologically, and compared them with the dates in our battalion history booklet, I realized I had become a world-class liar.

The anxiety of mothers is common to all mankind, but in the Jewish mother of that day it reached devotional proportions.

So, I lied.

After the "Night of Hell" I wrote:

....."Naturally, there is danger! But, isn't there danger walking up the stairs, crossing the street, riding in cars? I thought that surviving a season with the orchestra had shown you I could take care of myself. You remember, it eventually proved your fears were unfounded and more in your imagination than anything else? I didn't starve, I wasn't killed by a trombone slide and there weren't any cowboys and Indians in San Antonio, Texas.

"Please send me a package."

I was a congenital bicycle lover.

One day, I borrowed a bike from the house where we had set up an aid station and pedaled back to the last town we had occupied. It was a glorious down hill coast of about three kilometers.

As so often happened, I did not know that the Germans had reoccupied the land to the north of the road. They waited until I was straining on the rougher ride uphill before lobbing in the mortars. After that ride back, I would have won any Grand Prix bike championship.

I wrote:

".....You see, we are not in danger all of the time. Today, for example, I took a bike ride into the countryside. It was beautiful and exciting. I wish you would think of it as more of a camping trip out into the countryside.

"Please send me a package."

My mother wanted to feel that she was contributing to the war effort, so she was knitting socks that were even too large for Dutch and were so loosely knit that they left cyclone fence impression marks on my feet.

But, the most difficult things to handle were the foodstuffs she sent, things she was sure the Army wouldn't serve. Of course, they wouldn't! They needed us to stay alive to fight!

My worst lie of all, was the day after the SS incident on the mountainside:

".......From your letters, I can see that you are still worrying too much. I don't see why you are under the impression I am lying to you. I will admit that there are a lot of things I don't tell you about, but what I do tell you is true. We don't fight all of the time. We go back to rest often and we do things like bike riding and sight seeing.

"We have got the Germans on the run now. The hardest is to catch them. When we do, we give them hell!

"Please send me a package."

If there is an afterlife, I hope they write off lies against good intentions.

EXILE

It happened very soon.

B Company had been without a medic for the three weeks since Texas had been hit on the head by a mortar. The replacement from Division had not yet arrived.

Wilson wasted no time. The day after we returned from the mountain, Missouri, who was now replacing Adams as Sergeant, if you can believe that, advised me that I was getting the job and would be picked up by the B Company jeep the next day.

I was to know a few more like Missouri in my time, incompetents with little personal character, who worked their way up through an organization through personality and guile, currying the favor of superiors. Eventually, the truth reveals itself, or they lose their mentor and they nosedive into obscurity. But meanwhile, it was galling that a person of such high character and courage as Sgt. Adams was being replaced by a piss-ant like Missouri.

Ironically, while many people of character had fallen and were yet to fall before V.E. Day, Missouri never suffered a scratch. Wilson gave him some decorations and he seemed always to be the center of small groups, humorously relating his combat fantasies.

I found also that if one attempts to disabuse a believer of his admiration of such a person, one's self becomes the object their anger. No one wants it exposed that he has been "conned."

I would imagine that Missouri has spent the intervening years as the center piece of some American Legion or Veterans of Foreign Wars Post, called upon regularly to relate his humorous stories of personal heroism.

Even though I expected this assignment, I was still small-bore demolished. It was a form of being rejected by one's own family, intolerable as it may be. It reinforced the realization that in the Army as well as life, we rarely have free choice, but are pawns moved about by other forces.

Everyone in the aid station was avoiding my eyes that evening as I was gathering my few things together. I was to go out with nothing more than my medical kit bag, so all else went into my bedroll and duffle bag which remained with the station.

What hurt me most was Lawson's conduct. Now that I had fallen from grace in our tight little social circle, in his culture, it had become necessary for him to cut me loose, lest I drag him down, too. I had noticed recently that he was doing a lot more ass-kissing and false laughter with Captain Wilson, perhaps out of fear that the same fate might befall him.

Since Lawson had been reassigned by the time I had been recalled to the aid station after V.E. Day, our paths never crossed again until we met at the discharge center in the United States in April of 1946.

Lawson had filled out physically and looked very confident. We eyeballed each other's chests and determined privately, we had tied in the combat medals competition.

Lawson returned to his world of corporate "Society", and college fraternities, and I returned to the question of what I would do now that I was abandoning the world of music, which in the aftermath of my war experiences had become too trivial.

The last time I actually spoke with Lawson was when I enrolled at the Northwestern and looked him up at his fraternity house.

He was the vice-president-elect of that fraternity and showed me around graciously. Somehow he must have assumed that I was angling for a pledge bid, because he gratuitously said as I was leaving, "Well, you do know, we don't accept anyone but Protestants."

I was too stunned to answer. If I hadn't been, I would have told him that there was no way that I would ever join him, nor that bunch of adolescents running around naked inside, snapping towels at each other's asses.

I closed that chapter of my life!

As for Wilson, it was "out of my hair, out of my mind." I don't believe he gave me a second thought after he had made his decision.

When I was recalled to the station after V.E. Day, his jaw dropped a bit when I walked in. He seemed surprised that I had survived. "Hi there, fellah!" It was like our brand new meeting on the heights over Marseilles. "Nice having you back!"

Nice having me back you son-of-a-bitch! What you really mean is, you never expected me to make it back. But, I did survive, you bastard, if only to put a momentary bone in your throat.

I wasn't afraid of him anymore, and he knew it. There was no more he could do to me after V.E. Day. He had lost his power.

WELCOME ABOARD!

Shakespeare indicates in Hamlet that we are more likely to hang on to the woes we have than venture into the woes of which we know not.

When the Baker Company jeep pulled up to the aid station the next morning, everyone busied himself elsewhere, except Shapiro who risked the Captain's wrath by walking out with me.

"Grossman told me about what you did on the mountain top. You'll make it!" His face looked pained, like a man who had not come to terms with the compromises he had been making because of his own fears. I detected tears rising.

"You've been a good friend, Shapiro." I realized he was catching sobs, so I jumped in the jeep: "Home, James!"

We took off. I rode in thought and silence.

If I had been concerned about changing families, I was wrong! The reception I received at Baker Company was overwhelming. They were clearly happy to see me again. The few days on the mountain top had bonded us all.

Sgt. Riley came out to give me great big Irish bear hug.

I had status and acceptance. I had real family.

The lesson was learned! Don't judge yourself until you judge your family or social setting. If you can't change the latter, go somewhere else where you are appreciated for what you are, not what they want you to be.

I was happy!

A New Life

Once realized, we sometimes wonder why we feared change.

Removed from the repressive atmosphere of the Captain's world, I expanded psychologically.

Natural leadership talents emerged. I was never one to seize leadership but if circumstances thrust such upon me, I would perform.

In fact, for me it kicked into a cocked hat the theory of the "indispensable man." For the longest time, most of us had agonized about what would happen if we lost Captain Coburn or Captain Brown, or some non-commissioned officer upon whom we had come to rely.

What happened?

Nothing! The next in line or some other subordinate figure would step right up and become the new "indispensable man." This lesson stuck with me for a lifetime, and I never again subscribed to that theory.

Since, Lt. Anderson had not yet been replaced, Sgt. Stacy was acting officer, but I found that because of my combat experience and general knowledge of tactics from my ROTC days, many decisions were made in conference between Stacy, Riley and myself.

In fact, we three would generally meet as a group with the commissioned officers of the other companies.

Combat kicks the hell out of the rigidity of official rank. Competence and experience establish an ad hoc pecking order.

When we were later provided with an officer who had been snatched as a replacement from an accountant's desk at Seventh Army, he was wise enough to stay in the background and sign the proper requisition forms and report papers. At tactical pow-wows he would stand a few steps away watching and listening.

We were subject to no more, what you would call, "confrontational battles." The Germans were retreating. I really don't know where they were going, except the theory was they were going to put up a last defense in a redoubt in Bavaria.

What we were encountering now were "catch up" skirmishes where, for the first time, major casualties were not primarily from heavy, medium and light ordinance, but from small arms fire.

Tactical field maneuvering was the order of the day, and I was good at that. Since, I could not officially carry a gun, one of the riflemen carried an officer's carbine for me in case of need.

We did a lot of overland marching and vehicle-borne site jumping. All that we had was what we could carry, and our sleeping arrangement were wherever we could find them.

Since casualties were rarer now, combat had become more of an adventure and that pleased me.

The officers of the other companies couldn't have been nicer to me. There was no such crap as saluting. Beside Captain Coburn, there was Captain Perkins, a "90-day wonder" businessman from the South whose big practical joke was to get his jeep driver to pretend trying to run me down when they pulled up.

The commander of Company D represented an object lesson to me in reverse discrimination. Despite the fact that he was a graduate of West Point, a movie model of what a West Point graduate should be and an excellent officer, he had been blocked in his advancement in rank by the fact that the entire regiment was dominated by non-professional officers. He was still a First Lieutenant doing a Captain's job.

I called him Lt. West Point and no one was more pleased than I when after V.E. Day he was rapidly promoted up to the ranks he deserved.

TANKS FOR THE MEMORY

Toward the end, the Germans were retreating so fast that we were using any mode of transportation available to keep up with them, even tanks.

We would load maybe ten of us onto the tops of each of a string of tanks rumbling down the roads. There, I witnessed some of the dumbest conduct ever.

The first thing I would do was slip my medical bag strap over some immovable object such as an antenna rod, because the rumbling vibration of the tank plus our exhaustion guaranteed our dropping off to sleep.

Some guys sat right at the edges where they were falling off right and left, and occasionally in front or back. It is not pleasant seeing a man pressed with his suit on.

Occasionally, they would fall asleep with their M1 safety catches off and their guns would go off.

One time the enemy set off a barrage of "screaming mimmies" at the tank parade, the most harrowing sound of rockets imaginable and while we jumped off trying to find places to hide, the tankers, serene in their secure interiors, blithely rumbled on with most of our equipment aboard.

We had to do a special marathon to catch up with them and then try not lose our legs to the tracks as we clambered aboard again.

All in all, the next time we had trucks, some of the guys kissed the hood ornament before they climbed aboard.

JOTTINGS

We were on one side of a river digging in when a sniper took a shot at one of our guys who was using a slit trench.

He got mad and shot back.

In no time we had a full-scale exchange, including mortars.

Regiment was advised by radio of the engagement from both sides of the river.

Captain Coburn came running out of the message center: "Stop! Stop! That's our boys over there!"

In fifteen minutes of this crossfire, not one person had been hit, which makes one wonder about our accuracy.

If our boys had been better shots, we would have had a lot of casualties that day.

• • •

Hawkins, was one of our Company sharpshooter-snipers.

We had a rest break along a beautiful stream.

He had this big telescopic site on an old Springfield 03 bolt-action rifle and he was scanning the opposite shore.

We had just had K-rations and I was lying on my back gazing at the clouds, when he said: "Uh Oh!"

I turned over to look. "What do you see?"

He was setting up his elbows to fire: "There's a German taking a piss over there."

I looked and sure enough!

He squeezed off a shot and the guy bent over, and jumped up and down holding his crotch area.

"Hawkins! You didn't?"

Urban rushed over. "Is he dead?"

Hawkins pulled the bolt and shot another bullet into the chamber: "No, he isn't, but he might as well be!"

I always had a lot of trouble dealing with the latent perversity in some of our boys.

• • •

We were way out ahead of our supply people and had nothing but K- and C-rations for days.

One of our country boys, Burson, jumped up. "I can't stand another K-ration. Start a fire!"

"What the hell are we going to cook?" asked Harold.

"What do you think? Fish!"

"We don't have any lines or hooks. How are we going to catch enough for this bunch?"

Burson walked down to the edge of the stream, pulled the pin on a hand grenade and lobbed it in. There was a muffled sound and a big bubble ripple that spread toward the shores. Very shortly stunned fish began rising to the surface.

Burson returned: "You scoop them up Harold. I'll start the fire.

Those country boys never ceased to amaze me.

MACHINE GUN KELLY

When Company B First Sgt. Stacy left to accept a battlefield commission, first platoon Sgt. Riley became acting first sergeant and Corporal Kelly moved up to acting platoon sergeant.

It is hard to describe Kelly, a reticent young man from the plains of Kansas.

He was gaunt and tall like the actor Jimmy Stewart, but the body was topped by a very large lantern-jawed head that tended to look like a naked skull under his steel helmet. He didn't walk, he strode.

At first I thought he lacked intelligence, but I soon learned, though he listened with immobile facial muscles, he understood and executed every nuance of his assignments.

When he became corporal of the third squad, he traded his M1 rifle for an officer's carbine. When he became platoon sergeant he traded his carbine for an officer's 45 Colt automatic, and one time when we were riding tanks to a new destination, he traded the 45 with a tanker for a Thompson machine gun, the kind used by the FBI and Chicago gangsters.

That afternoon he practiced shooting into a mound of dirt. Knowing the tendency of tommy gun muzzles to pull up when bursts were fired, he learned to spray horizontally.

This became very handy, because we were now primarily clearing wooded areas, and I was unable to break our guys of the habit of firing off all of their magazines at one time when we were fired upon.

This created a lull while they were all reloading at the same time, during which the enemy could rise again and let us, or the flanking units, have it.

I worked out a pattern where Riley, with his Browning automatic rifle, Kelly, with his Thompson machine gun, and I with a carbine would hold fire until our guys mindlessly blew their wads and then we would commence firing as they were reloading.

It worked and we didn't lose any men.

But, this one time, nothing seemed to work. We were pinned down and the enemy was not letting us move anywhere. Riley and I decided we had better hunker down and hope that one of our other platoons would find and relieve us.

One replacement rifleman decided to shoot a grenade off of his rifle grenade launcher, which was idiotic, since we were in a wooded area. What was worse, instead of poking the butt of the rifle into the ground and holding it down with his foot as he was taught, he decided to shoot it from his shoulder, which of course, not only knocked him down, but broke his shoulder.

The grenade hit a tree limb and bounced back toward us. We all ducked and the fragments went over our heads.

"Fuck this shit!" That was the longest sentence I ever heard Kelly speak.

He got up from behind a log, and strode, remember I said he didn't walk, toward the German positions spraying horizontally with his Thompson machine gun. The other guys, seeing him move, jumped up and followed him, shooting.

There was hardly a shot from the other side and we didn't have a single casualty. The German's were standing up in their foxholes with hands raised, shouting: "Wir Geben sich Auf!"

When they were gathered up, they looked with deathly fright at Kelly.

How would you have felt if you saw that gaunt "Specter of Death" striding at you across a field spraying machine gun bullets?

My Hero?

I was becoming really confused.

What I perceived as normal combat conduct was resulting in officers telling me that they were putting me in for decorations.

Since Grossman had told them that Capt. Wilson would block anything put through the normal channels of the aid station, they were sending up the citations through their own companies.

I was having difficulty seeing myself as a hero. Sgt. Bruce could have become a hero had he not tried so hard to be. Fitzpatrick was a hero. They both presented the proper image. But, me? I was just a skinny apartment-dwelling kid from just north of the Union Stockyards in Chicago, one year removed from high school.

But, then again, we all were kids. Our junior officers were just out of college and our Captains and Majors in their early thirties.

What's more most of us didn't think we were doing anything special. But, what the hell! If the Army could give medals to our Generals just for visiting the front, then why not throw a few our way? Little did we know that each medal would later count 5 points toward the total needed to get on a ship back home.

ATROCITY

One day, we had a messy engagement and lost two men who were original members of the company from the States.

The whole Company was in a rage, and when seven German prisoners, scared shitless in their ragged Wehrmacht uniforms, were marched into the farm yard where we were resting, I was really concerned with the mood of our boys.

The prisoners were the standard issue for the times, four very young and three old, the left-over talent of the Reich. Our guys were kicking them and pushing them around.

The young ones, perhaps seeing my red cross, were shooting me shy, tentative hopeful smiles, while the older ones looked downward in resignation.

"Put them in the barn 'til we can get them to the rear," said Riley. They were marched out of sight around the farmhouse.

Riley, myself, and some others turned back to this little fire where we were heating up C-rations, when shots rang out from the rear. Riley jumped up and ran around the back with the others. I was afraid to go.

I sat there with my heart pounding. Finally, I got up and walked slowly around to the rear.

"They're all dead," said Riley.

"They tried to get away," lied one.

I looked down at the young boys scattered about the yard. They had looked at me so hopefully just a few moments ago. I had let them down. My heart was cracking. My throat was constricted. I could hardly breath or get a word out.

At once, I exploded. My throat opened up and I screamed: "We don't kill prisoners! We don't kill prisoners!" I was jumping up and down like a kangaroo, repeating the phrase over and over again!

Everyone was looking at me as if I belonged in a psycho ward.

Riley grabbed hold of my shoulders and was trying to hold me down. Finally, I stabilized. I was standing there with short sobs.

Nicholson tried to placate me: "My God, what are you so excited about? They killed Mancini and Roberts....."

"We don't kill prisoners!"

"Why?"

"Cause that's what Nazis do! We're Americans! We do not kill prisoners!"

There was dead silence, then someone shot the Coup de Gras: "After all Whitey, you were best friends with Mancini."

"Don't give me that fucking friendship crap! Don't let them drag us down into the shit with them! That's what we're fighting about. We're better than them! We don't kill prisoners!" I screamed.

Then, I turned and buried my head on Riley's shoulder. I was sobbing: "They don't understand, Riley. They just don't understand."

LET MY PEOPLE GO

In one of those coincidences that generally happen only in movies, we overran the American prisoner camp that contained each and every one of our medical group that had been captured since we crossed into Germany in January, including Lt. Herman, Sgt. Adams and Whitmore.

We were all ecstatic that evening, and into the next day when they were to be processed for return to the States.

By mid-morning, I was rebelling against their non-stop recitations of the misery and indignities they had endured with their long marches, constant relocations and terrible food.

My sympathy ran out: "You took long marches; we took long marches. You slept in lousy places; we slept in foxholes. You ate lousy food; we ate lousy food. But, you are all alive, un-wounded and healthy. You're going home; we're still fighting. Look at what is left of us! Johnson was mince-meated by a land mine, Friedman and Harris got slaughtered in their foxhole," and I continued with the list of the dead and wounded. As a matter of fact I was just about the last of the original group.

They looked very hurt that I was not completely empathetic with the miseries they had endured, but, then again, they weren't appreciative of mine.

Lt. Herman wrote a humble letter of apology to Captain Wilson for all the inconvenience he had caused him, especially having himself, Adams and Whitmore captured. He gave it to me to deliver to Wilson.

Poor, kind, simple-hearted Herman! He didn't have the slightest clue that being captured was the best gift he could have given Wilson.

I dumped the letter into a slit trench.

THE MOUTH IS MIGHTIER

I received one decoration which was written up much more seriously than I took it to be.

In the last week before V.E. Day, we reached this small town at the bend of the Danube River.

There was a train trestle bordering the town, pocked by some openings to the farm fields on the other side.

The trestle was a natural defensive position, so the companies arrayed themselves along about a half mile stretch with guns poked over the top like it was an old American Civil War parapet. We knew the last of the Germans were out there, somewhere.

The train station was turned in a H.Q. and I was there with several of the officers when a rifleman brought in a Polish slave laborer whose wife had been wounded and was now in a small railroad workhouse about a half mile out in No Mans Land.

The officers looked at me and I said, "O.K., I'll go!"

Captain Coburn called over two of his platoon sergeants who had Thompson sub-machine guns to go with us. The Sergeants didn't seem too happy about this development.

When we got to the nearest trestle opening, one Sergeant said quite simply, "Shit! I ain't going out and gettin' killed for no Polack lady!" and they turned around and went back.

I shrugged and walk the half mile with the poor Polish worker.

Actually, the woman was more frightened than hurt, and while I was putting the bandage on the nasty gash on her side, I saw some German jack boots out of the corner of my eye. Then, I heard them discussing what to do with me. I was keenly listening to hear whether death was a serious option.

Finally, I had to look up, and found that there were three of them. I was relieved to see that they were Wehrmacht, not SS.

Knowing that Germans are inclined to submit to authority, I got up and said in my most guttural German dialect: "Give this man your guns and give me your valuables. I'll see that you get them back on the other side."

They looked bewildered: "But, you are our prisoner!"

So, I went into my best speech about how the war was almost over, why die, food's good on the other side, etc.

Finally, they shrugged, gave their rifles and pistols to the Polish man (who told me later that he had fully expected to die) and their wristwatches, wallets, photos, etc. to me which I put in my medical bag. (Yes, I did give these back to them after they went through the "liberation" screening by our troops.)

The scene was out of a movie. Three German soldiers (two of them carrying a wounded woman), one shabby Polish worker, and one skinny soldier with a red cross on his helmet walking across No Man's Land toward a distant parapet bristling with the rifles, 30 caliber machine guns and mortars of a full battalion of American soldiers backed up by a fleet of tanks.

The absurdity of the situation was not lost on me.

As far as the reception, you would have thought I had captured the whole German Army.

Captain Coburn said: "If it hadn't been you, Whitey, I wouldn't have believed it."

P.S. The two sergeants got their asses reamed.

In later years, my family found my citations and had them framed and put on the wall.

I found my nine year old son looking up this particular one with his hands clasped behind his back.

"Dad, was it true that they were armed and you weren't?"

"That's true!"

"And....all you had going for you was that you could talk to them?"

"That's true!" I sensed the first stirring of respect.

"Dad, those poor guys never had a chance!"

DER FUHRER IST TOD!

On May 2nd, I wrote this letter home:

"Last night about 10;00, we were sitting around the radio listening to some German music and talking about the war, when some German Admiral came on and in German told the German people that Hitler was dead. Well, it didn't make much difference to us anyway. We expect this war to be over very soon. Now, we are wondering what's next. It's a toss-up whether we will go to the Pacific, or be occupation troops. I would much rather like to do the last."

So, do a nineteen year old and his buddies dismiss the death of the single most evil figure of our century.

All the horrors committed at his direction were yet to be revealed. They were far greater than even our own propagandist's wildest exaggerations.

For years afterward I needed to tolerate the Germans and German-Americans who were in denial of the very truths I witnessed with my own eyes at the concentration camp at Dachau.

These were so horrible, that I am still unable to write of them now, even after sixty-two years.

V. E. Day

On May 7, 1945, V.E.Day, I walked alone to a stream nearby and took a photo of myself kneeling and looking into the water.

I still looked a very young 19 years old on the outside, but I was a lot older on the inside.

I had endured the "Trial by Fire". My untested courage had prevailed.

I had been through the worst of combat without ever having physically hurt a single soul.

I had not needed a gun to prove myself "macho" -- just a little medical bag and a litter.

As I wrote to my family on that little river bank that day:

> "No one can tell me how it is to freeze, because I have been cold. No one can tell me how it is to be scared because I have been scared. No one can tell me why you should respect the rights of other men because my life has depended upon them and no one can tell me they are a better man than I because I have proven to them and more importantly to myself that I am just as good, if not better.
>
> "When there was a better leader, I followed and when there wasn't, I led. Not seldom were the times when upon me depended the lives of many.
>
> "So you see, I am not complaining about my lot in the Army. As long as I must be in it, I have made the most of it.
>
> "I am not afraid of anything anymore because the worst that could happen to me has already happened. All I have to look forward to from now on is a happier day.
>
> "It's an experience that I am not sorry I had, but, would never want to have again." ---- nor my children, nor anyone else's children, for that matter.
> Love,
> Your son

A SHOT IN THE DARK

We like to think we do not have long term effects from combat, but some things get programmed in despite ourselves.

We learned early on, if one hears a shot, he breaks at the knees quickly and heads for the dirt.

This can mean bruised ribs if you fall on your equipment, but better bruised than dead.

One night, about a week after V.E. Day, the Special Services boys commandeered a local movie house and showed a new Gary Cooper cowboy release.

Not knowing whether we would be getting civilian or returning soldier resistance, we were still fully armed, and it made for some crowded seating, but, we were happy for the diversion.

At about the half way point in the feature, this good guy goes into a cabin at night looking for something. It was very quiet and only moonlight lit up the room. He spots a box under the window and lifts the lid.

Suddenly, a very loud shot rang out in the theater.

There was a terrible crashing of guns and equipment as everyone dropped to the floor.

Then, there was silence.

Finally, I lifted my head above seat top level. Instead of a battalion of infantry, there was an empty theater.

Slowly, M1 rifles were being leveled across seat tops and some guys began prone crawls down the aisles, searching out the sniper.

Nobody, except me was looking at the screen where it was developing that some bad guy had shot our good guy through the window above the box.

"All clear!" I yelled.

Bodies began to show above seat levels and we were universally embarrassed.

The most common remark was: "I knew it wasn't a sniper!"

All that I knew was that I was still trembling.

These involuntary reactions hang on for years.

I was walking down La Salle street in Chicago in a business suit in the days when automobiles were still commonly backfiring.

I found myself on the ground surrounded by the well-panted legs of a number of the curious.

I picked myself up.

"Just looking for my contact lens," I lied.

RILEY

Sergeant Riley, Company B First Sergeant, was one of the most endearing people I have ever known. He knew nothing but smiles and laughter, no matter how severe the conditions. His personal courage was unquestionable. His appeal to women was unmatched, except perhaps by John Fitzgerald Kennedy.

General consensus, however, was that he was born with an extra set of gonads.

He was like an Irish bloodhound sniffing out the local bawdy houses for the whole regiment.

He was able to find non-professional sex during the most intense combat conditions. It was not at all unusual to see him emerging from a nearby stube, kissing the fraulein or frau goodbye as we were moving on to new positions. There are probably a brigade of smiling Irish-German children, fully grown by now, in the tracks left by Sergeant Riley.

He loved me like a brother, or a son, and he was intensely disappointed that I didn't share his addiction to non-stop sex. He did everything he could to initiate me into the "Wide World of Eros."

I did everything I could do to keep him out of the brig.

I was never able to get him to internalize that fraternizing with enemy civilians was a military code violation punishable by loss of rank and imprisonment.

Since he was the company sergeant and I was the medic, we bunked together, so we were rarely separated.

Two weeks after V.E. Day, we were sharing this little first floor hotel room in a charming village on the Neckar River.

I say sharing, but, the reality was, he had found himself a "snapper", his highest sexual accolade, and I had to cover for him every night.

One morning at about 5 AM., there was an anxious rapping at the window. There stood Riley stark naked and shivering in the morning chill.

His "snapper's" husband, a German army Major, had been mustered out and arrived during the morning hours.

Riley jumped through the window.

Now, the dilemma! We still had only combat issue, only one set of everything, and Riley had to front Reveille at 7:00 AM.

I had no choice! In the growing dawn, I marched to the "snapper's" house, a little stube at the end of the street, fully expecting to be the Seventh Army's first post-combat casualty.

He threw open the door violently. His Teutonic features reddened, and I thought he was going to strike.

He looked under his raised arm and down my skinny frame from red-crossed top to the army-booted bottom, and shook his head slowly. Certainly, his wife would substitute better than this for him in bed.

I said in German: "Excuse me! I have come for my comrade's clothes." He looked at me for a moment, then swung the door open slowly, and let me pass.

The frau was propped up in the bed, comforter pulled up to her chin, tear marks still showing on her rosy cheeks.

"Guten Morgen!" I said as I tipped my helmet.

"Guten Morgen!" she said softly. I gathered the clothing under my left arm.

The Major was still holding open the door. I passed him and turned on the stoop. "Danker shoen, Herr Major", and I saluted.

He started to salute before he realized the absurdity of the situation. Instead, he slammed the door.

Several weeks later, I was called back to my medical unit and sadly parted with Riley.

About a month later I suffered food poisoning. By the time the ambulance got me to the field hospital in Baden-Baden, I was unconscious.

The next morning, when my eyes opened and focused I was greeted by the spectacle of a naked man on knees and elbows have his posterior probed by an army doctor.

I sat up shocked: "What the hell is this?"

"This is a VD ward, that's what it is!" replied the doctor.

The physiological improbability of me being in a VD ward is incalculable: "How could I be in a VD ward?"

The nurse pushed me back down: "There were no other beds last night!"

I slunk around for several days, hoping no one I knew would see me, when:

"Whitey!"

There was no mistaking it! It was Riley at the other end of the hall.

He raced down to embrace me: "I am so proud of you! I knew you could do it! I knew you could do it!"

He dragged me down to his ward, and proudly introduced me to all of his fraternity of pro-kit rejecters.

There was no father more proud of his son, no brother more gratified at having passed the torch.

At the first chance, I raced down to my end of the hall and buttonholed my nurse: "Please don't tell him I don't have VD! Please don't tell him I don't have VD!"

"OK! OK!"

She briefed me on the treatment procedures and I sauntered casually back to Riley's ward.

"Was she a `snapper'?"

"The best!"

"Hear that, guys?" He squeezed my knee.

The next day I was discharged and slipped out of the back door of the hospital. The nurse promised not to snitch.

I never saw Riley again.

Part III
The Aftermath

Part III

The Aftermath

ON TO JAPAN

There were many rumors regarding the future of our division, the most persuasive of which was that we would be returning to the United States for a furlough and then on to the Pacific Theater.

In preparation for this, we were doing tactical exercises in the field for a different type of warfare.

Because Japan had not signed the Geneva Convention, medical aidmen were issued officer's carbines and I was now doing legitimately what I had been doing surreptitiously before.

The most painful thing we were experiencing now were the little German children who were being killed and wounded playing in uncleared mine fields and with unexploded ordinance. We were channeling these through our aid station, and working on such miniature bodies seemed to be a mockery of the consequences of war.

It always bothers me when the little innocents of any nation suffer for the actions of the adults. I am unable to project guilt unto the next generations.

Other than that, if you can imagine this, we were trying to save the German civilians lives from the backlash to their own country's rampage.

The Eastern prisoners of war and slave laborers were free and on the loose and we were busy rounding them up and putting them back behind barbed wire fences again.

ALLES KAPUT!

The most defining population characteristic in our part of Germany in the aftermath of hostilities was enormous self-pity.

In retrospect, I cannot bring myself to think that they all knew what awful mayhem their armies had visited upon their conquered and in the death camps, anymore than American citizens knew what was really going on in Viet Nam. I cannot buy the proposition of collective guilt and punishment.

But, for those who will be satiated only by the most extreme of retribution, be advised, that due to the allied bombings in the 10,000 plane raids, most of the German cities were in ruins.

One Italian movie director called it "Germany Year Zero" and for the heart of Germany, he was right.

The most common phrase was: "Alles kaput!" The closest English translation would probably be: "All destroyed" but that doesn't suck all of the implications out of that German idiom.

They probably know now how badly their military "kaputed" most of Eastern Europe, Russia, and sundry other lands, but at that time they could only look inward.

The slave laborers and prisoners of war that poured out of the prison camps knew, however, and they set up a reign of terror that "kaputed" many German lives and buildings before our army was called in to corral them and put them behind fences again until they could be repatriated.

Meanwhile, I was assigned to be the "kaput" arbitrator for several local villages. Since, all effective municipal administration had ended, the local citizenry were bickering themselves into civil war.

I had to settle some serious "kaput" problems, such as, "Aunt Sophie took the only bed when your troops moved into our first floor and we were homelessed into our attic."

What I really wanted to do was to drag them back to France to show them how many attics and homes were "kaputed" there, but I was now a member of the diplomatic corps.

They became much more muted and somber as their soldiers straggled back and advise them of how "un-kaputed" they really were.

What was hurting me now, was the string of young children who were blowing themselves up playing with unexploded shells and mortars, or wandering off into uncleared mine fields. Those were valid "kaputs".

THE JUDGMENT

Recently, I was empaneled as a potential juror.

The defendant had already pleaded guilty to killing a person. The facts were not in dispute.

The jury was only to be asked what degree of a killing it was: first, second, manslaughter, et cetera. so that the judge could determine what sentencing formula he should apply.

The defendant, a male, was neat, clean, presentable, affable, almost endearing, a quintessential all-American boy, who looked like he could hurt no one.

As the evidence commenced, a picture was building of one of the most horribly executed murders I have ever heard about. The jurors were turning white and I had to leave in nausea. I won't give you the details.

That was my growing feeling about Germany as the evidence started to come in. The other Europeans trapped in the country were appalled at how Americans were coddling and protecting their oppressors. They were beating upon us with information regarding what the German army had done to their countries.

The German's word for the East Europeans was "Schmutzig" (dirty). Well, I have known many such in my Chicago days and the last thing one could say about them is that they were dirty.

Americans generally don't like to hate, but some of us were in a true quandary about how we should feel.

"Nicht Nazi!"

The term "Nicht Nazi!" was running neck in neck with the already established, "Alles Kaput!"

It seems that every living Nazi in Germany miraculously disappeared on V.E. Day.

If you walked into a store, especially if you were carrying a weapon, the owner would waggle his arms and exclaim: "Nicht Nazi!"

Everybody's "shack" fraulein and their families were "Nicht Nazi!"

Nobody was Nazi!

How did Hitler almost conquer most of Europe if all of the German people were "Nicht Nazi!"?

I became irresistibly drawn to the question, how did this nation become seduced by a man our propaganda depicted as a raving maniac?

It wasn't hard to find the answer. All I had to do was search the mountainous piles that our own "liberators" left in the middle of the floors of the apartments and homes of Germany.

There, I found the photos and literature distributed to the Deutcher Volk. This was not a strutting figure with the vicious countenance of our images, but, a gentle, benevolent face of a loving father figure, bending over to kiss children, grasping the hands of adoring women, wearing a suit and coat with a soft hat on his head.

I found beautifully written stories by Joseph Goebbels of Hitler's visits to various parts of the country to consort with his "volk."

He was our loving father, our leader (fuhrer) whose life was dedicated to our welfare and saving us from the evil forces that were boring in upon us.

I found myself becoming seduced.

It resulted in my unremitting hatred of "image makers" and ultimately made the Reagan Administration an eight year nightmare for me.

I was beginning to understand those pathetic "Alles Kaput!" villagers out there, but I was still having problems with the "Nicht Nazis!"

I became ambivalent. At times, I was in rage and hatred when more information about the death camps began to surface. At other times, as I met people of character, such as a flute teacher in Karlsrue, I was angry at myself for assessing collective guilt.

Finally, I shifted into neutral and decided to judge on a case by case basis.

But, I was a lousy judge!

In the Fall of 1947, while I was a student at Northwestern University, it was revealed that the school had hired for its German Department an American-born defector to Hitler's Germany, who had already renounced his American citizenship.

I was stunned! I was in my second quarter of study with this "all-American" guy that every student in the class loved. He was a great teacher, fair and easy going, and besides was grading me A.

I went to his office to offer my help.

He related how he had been a student in Germany when he was trapped by the war, and in order to save himself from starving, he needed to renounce his American citizenship to obtain employment.

No one, including the U. S. government, claimed that he had done more than work in a Berlin radio station as a translator and English language broadcaster of German news.

That was enough for me! I was ready to go to bat.

He must have misjudged my German sounding last name, because then, he gratuitously continued: "Of course, you know that Hitler is being lied about. He was a great man!"

My jaw dropped.

From a well modulated conversational tone, his voice began to rise in pitch and volume as he went through the well established catechism of Hitler's value to mankind! By the end of the recitation he was on his feet, having reached a climax rivalling the end of a Hitler speech.

There was silence.

"Herr Professor! You do know that I am Jewish, do you not?"

His jaw dropped to the floor. As he looked at me, his face softened.

His voice took on an entirely different, almost pleading tone: "I was born

in America! My newborn son was born in America! I am an American!"
Like hell you are, you son of bitch! You're another "Nicht Nazi!"

FRIEND OR ENEMY?

After V. E. Day, the Russian Army set up contact stations in various cities of Germany to facilitate the return of their nationals.

I was asked to work with a unit in Karlsrue, because while they could speak no English and we could speak no Russian, we could communicate in German.

The Russians at that time were our great heroes and friends.

Each morning for three weeks I would go to their small apartment several blocks from our billet, where I was greeted like a long lost brother, and had tea, eternal tea, thrust upon me from the ubiquitous samovars.

Because my name was German sounding, I gave them my nickname, "Whitey."

They loved "Vittey" and I loved them.

The contrast between them and the Germans was like manic versus depressive. They were upbeat and happy and when we went to the temporary enclosures where their people were awaiting repatriation, the internees would be singing lustily in great harmonies.

We were happy and great friends, until the word came down to me: Stay away from the Russians. Somehow, something had happened. We were now enemies.

They were very hurt when I avoided them on the street, and as a matter of fact I was as bewildered as they.

My masters and their masters had decided we were enemies, and like the Germans, we obeyed.

BREAKING UP IS HARD TO DO

On June 20th, 1945, I wrote:

"Dear Mother and Dad:

"I am afraid I shall have to tell you something that has struck me with the blow of a hammer. It is official now that our Division is to be broken up. Why? I don't know. Even appeals to Eisenhower have been futile.

"Why does it strike me so hard? I'll never forget the Company Commander (Coburn) who broke down crying as he told us this morning. Yes, the few of us left can tell you why. They can tell you of the boys that aren't here to be told. They can tell you of the close knit friendship that exists between we who have made it through to the end. Officers and men. They can tell you of the many things we have been through. All of the funny little things that happened. Hundreds of little things that make us all the more feel badly that we must now break up and go to different outfits. Start all over again with new people, make new friends. Instead of being the old men, to be the new men. Another thing that hurts is the fact that I was next in line for promotion, next even in line for pass.

"Maybe, in a few days I will feel better and make the best of it. But, meanwhile you know I don't feel so hot."

What I didn't talk about was how citizens from incredibly diverse regions, cultures, and religions had molded into "families" with severe fathers, like Wilson, nurturing fathers like Herman, tough brothers, like Adams and Fitzpatrick, wise-assed cousins like Missouri, not so bright cousins like Peters, Dutch, Watters and so forth. Each contributed his strength and endangered us with their weaknesses.

There had been a bonding that would have been highly unlikely in peace time, that opened the doors to the communication required to pull the several States into a closer Union and for this period of time, the greatest nation in the world.

If anything, it had been the "Good War" in which few questioned the righteousness of the cause, and never left the bitter after-effects of a Viet Nam.

THE GENERALS

Like most Americans who were drafted to serve, I would like to think it was a matter of chance. I was at a qualifying age, in qualify health, during a period in which our country was at war.

I want to feel that I was selected to serve by a fairly administered system without some privileged sons escaping service.

I would like to think that our actual participation in combat was a decision made by impartial selection, fully understanding that by chance some will endure more severe conditions than others.

In other words, if our units were to be envisioned as pawns on the Headquarters strategy board, we would hope that it was by pure chance that we were selected for the most dangerous assignments.

But when we have knowledge or reason to believe that our General is pushing our pawn piece toward the decision makers constantly saying "Use Us! Use Us!" then we get pissed off.

Because these officers do not have their own safety at stake, it is only their own personal glory and promotion that motivates them.

They don't suffer the freezing pangs of winter in foxholes. They don't dodge shrapnel and bullets, but they do later stand at the head of the remnants and accept the citations and the glory.

We came to believe that our repeated spear pointing of advances was more than just chance.

We were outraged when the Brigadier General, second in command of the Division, received a bronze star for every time he visited the lines where we lived constantly. He was up to eleven medals the last time I counted. Utterly shameless!

One of our fellows calculated that on a comparative time service basis each of us should have in excess of 10,000 bronze star medals.

The only time I saw him on the line, he slid backwards under a tank for protection when a stray shell came in. In other words, he was the Missouri of the division staff.

I would like to think the stories of our commanding general pushing us forward for his own glory were like those rumors common in other divisions, but based on what one of his relatives, who was a line officer, told me, I had the strong suspicion that they were true.

As a result, when the news reached us that he had suffered a nervous breakdown when told of the breakup of our division, his vehicle to glory, there was very little sympathy in the ranks.

A FRIEND WHO MOVES TO HIGH PLACES

Henry Adams in his autobiography used a phrase that has explained certain puzzling incidents that dot all of our lives: "A friend who moves to high places is a friend lost!"

There was no one in Baker company who wasn't pleased when First Sergeant Stacy was selected for a battlefield commission. He was a good soldier and a Rock of Gibraltar in combat.

We were sorry to lose him when he was sent back for training but we understood the Army's policy to place such new officers with new commands.

So, you can imagine how delighted I was after V. E. day to spot him walking down the middle of the street toward me.

He was short, so in combat clothes he looked a little baggy at the bottom, but, in a trim officer's uniform, he really looked sharp.

I rushed forward to greet him with outstretched arms.

Within a few yards he shouted: "Halt!" I stopped.

"Attention, soldier!"

I thought he was joking.

"Salute!"

I looked more closely at him. He was a little high but not drunk.

"How are you doing, Stacy?"

"Lt. Stacy to you!" he said pointing at the single gold bar on his helmet. "Now, salute!"

I was beginning to realize he was serious. Passersby were stopping to note this confrontation in the middle of the street.

For three weeks as his company medic, I had shared foxholes, beds, food and danger with First Sergeant Stacy. Now, this?

"Stacy, what in the hell is wrong with you?"

"I am telling you to salute, soldier."

"Fuck you, Stacy!"

Stacy turned to the non-comprehending Germans: "Did you hear that?

You're witnesses! Insubordination!" He pulled out his 45 Colt and held it at his side. The Germans began scattering.

"Now, I am warning you for the last time, private, salute!"

I stood with hands on hip in a "Ricarrili" slouch.

He raised the pistol and pointed it at me. By now we were rapidly becoming the only ones on the street, like in a movie face off at Dry Gulch. But, it was more serious than that. I wasn't at all sure he wouldn't shoot.

My whole concept of self was at issue. I refuse to accept intimidation by manufactured aristocracies. I turned my back on him and retraced my steps. I heard him cock the hammer.

"Stop! I am warning you, stop, or I'll shoot, Whitey!"

After all that combat, what a way to die! I expected to get a slug in my back any second. But, it didn't come and I made the half block to the corner with him still shouting warnings.

As I turned to the left, I glanced back at him. At a distance it looked as if he were shaking his fists and crying in frustration.

I took off like a bat out of hell, made a couple of corner turns, and fell against a building, drenched in sweat. I had really thought Stacy was going to shoot.

Again, and again, through the years, my mind has gone back that incident.

Why do people like Stacy who move from one social strata to another demand the overt acknowledgement of their new status by members of the class they have left?

As a matter of fact, the military is a metaphor for that whole phenomenon.

There are the work-a-day enlisted men, with their foremen and supervisors (i.e., the non-coms) and a class of executives (commissioned officers).

Since this doesn't cover all situations (like college professors, scientists, middle management) there are specialist rankings, neither officers nor non-coms, but "warrant officers."

In the military these social and power distinctions are acutely delineated with uniforms, insignia, saluting, and other forms of recognition.

There is also the state of mind.

I have found that true officer, executive and natural leaders, in virtually every field in which I have engaged in later years, are far easier to befriend and speak with, far less demanding of deference symbolism, far more at ease with their status than the Stacys who join the class through accident or merit promotion.

So, I have had warmer relationships with Captain Coburn, Lt. Herman, West Point and others officers and later with great political figures, musicians, writers, entrepreneurs and high ranking executives, than with the strivingly ambitious or with the enlisted men with whom fate had bound me.

But, a newcomer like Stacy needed to put me, and others like me, down, in order to validate his new position and state of mind.

I needed to resist in order to retain my own sense of scale, position and worth in the world.

In other words, we were instant enemies!

For the first time, I came to realize, I was too educated and worldly to be comfortable with enlisted men, but not willing to play the political price for striving to officer-ship, and not a sufficient specialist to become a warrant officer.

These conditions did not vary much for the rest of my life.

I was a personality in limbo.

THE EVIL THAT MEN DO

There were some in the United States Army who were compulsive looters.

There were some who were systematic looters.

There were some who were selective looters.

The fact is, during combat, while for some men on the line, looting was an avocation, for others in support and supply positions it was the primary vocation.

It was not unusual to see a supply truck, ammunition tractor, or even tanks looking like the peddler's wagons of my youth.

Ponder this most basic of all logical syllogisms: All armies in war zones loot. The United States had an army in a war zone, therefore, the United States army looted.

Of course, the euphemism "liberate" was used, and the rationale was: "this is the enemy that is killing our guys" but the fact remains it was looting.

Armies since earliest time can go through any structure like a swarm of termites. To visit these interiors afterward is to view studied mayhem: drawers overturned with contents all over the floors. Photos, papers, books, and whatever else in enormous piles, sifted and rejected.

It is my conviction that fully one-fifth of the pelf of Hitler's Germany still resides in the basements, attics and store rooms of the United States.

All armies in war zones have rapists. The United States had an army in a war zone, therefore, the United States Army had rapists.

Many times troops were lined up helmet-less for raped ladies to inspect them more intensively than reviewing Generals.

Many times men were pulled, screaming denials, from the ranks.

The rationale: "These are the women of the men who are killing our guys," but, nevertheless, to the Army's credit, it was still called rape.

After hostilities, "black marketing" went from bush league to major league within a week.

There was virtually nothing you couldn't buy for you or your Fraulein.

Enterprising looting was now paying off.

The standard of exchange was not gold, it was not the dollar, nor the English pound. It was American cigarettes. One carton equaled twenty American dollars. That stood rock hard as the most stable currency in the entire world for the whole year that I remained in Germany.

Officers and men who had been entrepreneurs before joining the Army, returned to the open market economy with the driving efficiency the world revered as "American know-how."

The United States government put a cap on this immediately. One could not send more money home that he was paid in Army salary.

Lt. Collins, the most prolific black marketeer I ever knew laughed his soft southern laugh through his trim moustache at that: "The United States regulators have never issued a regulation that we cannot circumvent!"

Within weeks, I estimate about 10% of the troops were not only fraternizing but "shacking with the frauleins." While they were being converted to anti-Slavic, anti-Semitic and the other antis in which the Germans specialized, a goodly share of American overseas provisions were being sucked into German stomachs via the sex organs, often to the support and cheering of German families. Because no money passed hands it was not called prostitution.

As quid pro quo for this ad hoc international pact, the Germans reciprocated by showing the black marketeers where and how to squirrel away their profits in Germany until the coast was clear.

I do not wish to reflect on the genuine love affairs and marriages that resulted in German war brides. I refer only to the transient immoral doings that seem to follow all conflict.

It wasn't weeks before some American soldiers were mouthing comments about how nice and so much like Americans the German people were and how really evil, excluding the United States, of course, her enemies were.

BEYOND POLITICS

On the other hand there were innocent apolitical Germans who were as much victims of this war as the citizens of any invaded country.

I had purchased a beautiful wooden flute in Stuttgart. Wooden flutes are almost never used anymore, but it reminded me of my own beautiful wooden clarinet.

I had very little to do while waiting for reassignment to other units, so I took it out and tried to play it.

Somehow, I got the word that the principal flutist of the local symphony orchestra lived nearby and since the orchestra was now disbanded, he was out of work and needed the income from students.

I went to his apartment building. Most of the apartments were vacant and looted, or occupied by American troops.

This gentle gray-haired man answered the door and led me into his small, neat apartment which had somehow escaped the rapine of war.

It was like a small oasis of universal sanity in the midst of contemporary mayhem. There were pictures and pencil drawings of the great composers, Mozart, Puccini, Tchaikovsky, Bach, Vivaldi, and numerous others on the walls.

There was a bust of Beethoven on the piano.

There was a wooden filing case packed with the great music for flute, and orchestral scores open all over the tops of the bookcases and tables.

This man was confused and numbed by what the political leaders had done to his country and had retreated to the artifacts of his art, works that transcended the contemporary and reached for the universal.

For the next three weeks, three times a week, it became a healing shelter for me also. I paid him in cartons of cigarettes which at that time were far more valuable than money.

At first we never discussed anything but music. Drawing upon my classical woodwind training, by the end of that time I had become sufficiently proficient for us to undertake duets.

The man had a lovely tone and poured his heart into each duet we played.

As we became less formal, I discovered that he was alone. His wife had died as a result of an Allied bombing, and his only son had died on the Russian front.

He wasn't complaining, he was only bewildered.

At my last lesson with him, we tackled the Bach Double Violin Concerto on our flutes.

In the beautiful second movement, I was transported. All that existed for me was that exquisite melody that was filling that one small room and all else, all the hell outside, faded away.

We were beyond nationalities. We were beyond politics. We were on the universal plane of human commonality, art.

I believe it affected my teacher also, for when we finished the movement, he rose and walked slowly over to the photos of his wife and son and shook his head slightly.

Then, he turned to me: "In this land of Bach, how could all this have happened?"

I sat in frozen silence and I shook my head.

I put my instrument in its case and left, quietly.

The next morning I placed all my remaining cigarettes inside his vestibule door.

I never went back for another lesson. It was too painful for me to watch him suffer.

THE CAT

Because the members of our unit were being reassigned to other organizations, I was soon the only occupant of our apartment in an otherwise vacated building in Karlsrue.

Therefore, I was very happy to have a cat show up one day that had been abandoned by one of the previous tenants.

The Germans were very assiduous in their breeding of animals, so, she was exquisitely beautiful and loving.

I brought her scraps and milk from our mess. She took up residence in my billet.

I had never had a pet before.

I decided that I was going to train her to sit on my shoulder like a parrot as I walked about the apartment and to show her off in that way to the others. It was, purely, an ego trip.

I placed her on my shoulder. She was not comfortable sitting there, as I now know cats never normally would be, and when I turned, she would lose balance and fall off.

I was the master, therefore, I decided to use the punish and reward technique of training.

It is very painful for me, now, to describe what followed, and I can only weakly excuse it on the grounds that I was suffering constantly from the pain of an impacted wisdom tooth, a callousness and hardening directly related to the combat experience and loneliness.

In short, I was a bastard.

I spanked her quite hard.

She tried, she really tried, to stay on my shoulder and I would reward her with petting and food, and she would be happy and purring.

But, then, she would fall off and I would repeat the process.

By the third day, I had turned a calm and loving cat into a nervous uncertain animal.

She would leave and hide. I would bring her back to show her who was the boss. It was a process, which in retrospect, I must say, was purely pathological. The bald truth was that I was abusing her as some people abuse helpless children.

Finally, she escaped entirely and I couldn't find her.

About a week later, when I was returning from mess, I spotted her in the walkway of the adjoining building.

When I went to fetch her, she arched her back, snarled and the hair went up on her back. When I reached down to take her, she clawed me, but stood her ground.

I had succeeded in turning a beautiful, gentle, loving creature into a neurotic defensive animal.

Ever since, I have been in deep shame over the incident and wish I could go back to find her and beg her pardon.

But, by now, of course, she would be dead for at least 30 years.

So, if you are up there in Cat Heaven, "Beautiful Cat", as I am sure you must be, I would like to say: "Please forgive that young, arrogant boy who did not understand the hurt he was inflicting upon you. But, be advised you did not suffer in vain.

"I have done penance for lo these many years, petting and loving to death all animals short of grizzly bears and mountain lions.

"And, thank you for forcing me to realize that before I condemn others, I should remember: "The devil resides in all of us!"

Injured By Friendly Fire

I had a severe jaw pain that plagued me all through combat.

Several times when it became excruciating, I went to our dental center at Regiment. The examining Major each time chewed me up for malingering and trying to get off the line and sent me back with aspirins, of which I already had hundreds in my medical bag.

How many were the victims of these heroic defenders of front line service?

So, I went back to the line, convincing myself that jaws should always feel that way.

After hostilities ceased, there was no longer any reason why they should continue to refuse treatment. But, I made a mistake. I went to our own alcoholic company dentist, who admitted to us that coming from wealth he had become a dentist only because his family felt that "he should have something to do!"

What he found "to do" was to hack, dig, saw and chisel away at what proved to be an impacted wisdom until he put me in a field hospital, unconscious, with a mysterious bug that probably was squirreled away in his unsanitary tool chest.

Anyone who is too gung ho on pure socialized medicine should contemplate what it is to be the unwilling member of any system where incompetence is guaranteed prisoners for its medical or dental practice.

By that time I had jowls that were a straight line from the tip of my jaw to the collar bone. I could have won any "fat boy" contest on that attribute alone.

I awoke with the head of surgery and his staff around my bed contemplating a tracheotomy.

Sulfa was doing nothing. So the Colonel authorized the administering of a new wonder drug, penicillin, which was so expensive that my treatment ran four thousand dollars, big, big money in those days.

The problem for me was that it needed to be injected every three hours because there was no way then to suspend it in the body.

This was tolerable, except that it was administered at midnight, 3:00 AM and 6:00 AM by a sadistic lieutenant nurse.

She would slip the covers back ever so lightly, pull up my hospital gown gently, then stab my butt viciously.

A couple of times she hit a sciatic nerve and I was having trouble sitting and walking.

I couldn't sleep at night, watching for her, and my whole sleep pattern got totally screwed up.

The shriek in the night even had some of the other guys taking turns staying awake to watch for her and to warn me.

I finally appealed to my primary dentist, and he nodded knowingly. Her reputation had preceded me.

The next day, she was quietly transferred to another building.

Then entered "Massage Molly", a chubby, muscled nurse dedicated to the proposition that all patients needed a daily massage to prevent bed sores. Of course, the fact that all of us were generally healthy and hardly ever lay down during the day, did not deter her.

She was know to throw an unwilling rifleman down on the bed and strip off his pajamas.

If the patient dared to have an erection during the treatment, he was in danger of an amputation. She developed a technique for clapping the backs edges of her hands together that turned the staff of life into a weeping willow.

Some appreciated the sensual aspects of this and lay waiting quietly for her each day as if they were dying warriors, but not I.

When I saw her coming I raced out of the other door. I napped in the library. I dared not take a chance in my own bunk.

JAWS

Like Riley's VD ward, I was in the wrong neighborhood again. Because I was a dental problem, I was put in a ward with all fractured jaws.

With the exception of one jeep accident victim, they were all super-macho, super-healthy victims of drunken "punch outs." All had their jaws wired together and took meals through straws.

Because I was the only one in the ward who could eat solid foods, they had to squirrel me away in the Captain doctor's room for meals, for fear I would be lynched.

This Captain doctor was another one of those wealthy, "I had to do something" doctors, but I liked him. But, that was not my major problem.

Because they were able to form words only by using their lips, I had great difficulty understanding any of the other guys in the ward. If you can't understand them, join them. I began to adopt the dialect. I clamped my teeth together and spoke with only my lips. Interpersonal relationships improved markedly.

The second Sunday afternoon of my stay, I was reading a book on my bunk when I spied an officer examining the chart at the foot of my bed. Then, he walked over to my side.

"Why weren't you at Mass this morning?" My bleary eyes focused on the cross on his collar. He was also a Lt. Colonel. My jaws were still too stiff to answer.

He launched into a tirade that my broken jaw represented the wages of sin, that I had abandoned the mother church and was ignoring the precepts of love thy neighbor and some other things I don't remember.

Then he concluded with a thunderous: "I want to see you at Mass next Sunday morning!"

I nodded. You don't argue with the power of God and the United States Army focused in one man.

The next Sunday, I got the same tirade, except stronger.

In my adopted dialect I answered: "But, I'm not Kasholish, Fasher!"

He walked back to my chart, and turned it for me to see. I peered closer: "Dash wrong, Fasher! I'm Chewish!"

He looked terribly disappointed. Then he brightened. "Perhaps, I can interest you in a conversion?

THE LAST COMMAND

One night, a skinny young member of our "Jawbone Brigade" slipped out for a night on the town.

He returned the next morning really potted. The other guys were trying to control him because they did not want their occasional night stalkings exposed.

Having become the "leader of men" that I had, I confronted him while two behemoths were holding this 140 pounder by both arms trying to calm him down.

With my strongest command voice, I pointed at him and said: "OK, soldier! Cut out this shit and get into bed!"

It worked.....I thought. He stopped struggling, looked at me through bleary, blood shot eyes and then in a rising crescendo said: "No wun telsh me wot to doo!" And, with that he threw off the two 200 hundred pounders and went for my throat.

A 180 pounder blind-sided him with a tackle and another 200 pounder piled on. Everyone else piled on who could.

He was pulling out from under the pile when another guy grabbed me by the arm and hustled me into the hallway.

"Dat lil guy ish a killer! Lesh hope he forgesh wo hoppened when he shobers up!"

The next morning I saw him advancing upon my bed. My blood ran cold.

"Got a chigaresh, pal?"

I gave him the whole carton.

That was the last time I ever issued a command in the Seventh Army.

REBIRTH

The last week I was in the hospital, Detroit came to visit bearing my duffel bag and transfer orders. He and several others were being transferred to an ambulance company out of Rothenberg in Southern Germany. I was going to a gas warfare medical battalion.

All of my personal items, including the beautiful wooden flute I had purchased in Stuttgart had been pilfered by the time Detroit was able to pack my bag, so I became depressed at having lost some treasured mementos.

The day I was discharged was a sad parting with the guys in the ward. A month with new friends in the army is like a lifetime. It seemed as if clearly articulated English had become my second language and I needed to relearn my native tongue if I wished to communicate in the outer world.

And, "Outer World" is what it had become. Life in an institution is removed from the normal interaction of daily life.

A hospital has its own rhythm, its own purpose and its own social structure. Recuperating is like a return to the womb. Your needs are met, nothing is expected of you, so you just lie back, float and contemplate your navel.

For several days, I had been practicing my return to the outside. It was a jolt. The noises on the street, people bustling by as if you weren't there, dodging vehicles. I had the urge to remain in the womb where we spoke our own exclusive tongue.

JAWS STRIKE BACK

The week before I was discharged from the hospital, my favorite ward doctor was replaced without notice.

When I was sitting in my dentist's chair, I asked him about it.

"You didn't hear?"

It seems the reason "Needle Point Nurse Nancy" had been assigned night nurse in our ward for so long was that she and our ward doctor were having a sexual affair in his room.

When my dentist pulled strings to get rid of her, it put a crimp in their coitus.

One night when both were potted and he was returning her to the building across the way, they forgot about the empty swimming pool between.

They were now both hospitalized.

Now, when I was lugging my duffle bag down to transportation, I ran into both of them in hospital robes taking the sun on the front steps.

They seemed very glum and reluctant to respond to my expressions of get "well soon" and all that crap.

He finally rubber-lipped: "Dash awl right! Be bash shoon!"

My newly-freed jaw dropped.

Then, she turned her head and gave me a friendly big smile.

My God! Her jaws were wired shut, too!

EACH MAN'S WAR

When I arrived at my new assignment, I first realized what a gulf had grown between those who had served on the lines in combat and those in the rear areas.

There were several of these gas warfare medical units in the army set up very early in the war to cope with poison gas if it should be used. Since it never was, these battalion were never committed to battle.

The only brush this unit had with combat occurred one day while they were camped in Holland. One lonely German plane had looked them over and then decided to do a single strafing run down the main street of their tent city.

No one, nor anything of importance was hit, but to the 350 officers and men of that battalion that single run was "their war."

The eight of us who joined the unit from our aid station are certain that we heard the personal version of each and every one of the 350 officers, non-coms, and enlisted men, and I am also certain that in the United States this very day there are thousands of children, grandchildren and veteran's posts who have heard the story of "The Day We Were Strafed!"

Soon thereafter, the Stars and Stripes announced that the United States had dropped a super bomb on Japan and by September 2nd, Japan had surrendered.

This was a tremendous relief for all of us, because we had heard that the United States anticipated one million casualties in an invasion of Japan, and now we could be thinking of going home.

The total service points we had accumulated became more significant. In one year, I had acquired 48, but it took 138 to be among the first to be discharged. That meant that I was sure to be in the Army of Occupation until they reached down to my number.

That was O.K. with me, because I still planned on seeing the great cities of Europe, a dream that was constantly thwarted, as you soon shall see.

That dream seemed closer to fulfillment because the gas warfare medical battalion had been activated for so long that the whole unit was eligible for discharge and I was reassigned to join Detroit and the medical ambulance unit in Rothenberg.

GRANNY MOSES

A jeep picked me up and took me to a transfer point some fifty kilometers away. It was just a couple of buildings with beds that the Army had appropriated.

As it happened, I was the only transferee there for the three days it took for my next transportation to arrive.

There was a young "gofer" working around the place. He was a Polish boy left over when the tide receded. He tried speaking English, but we ultimately fell back into the more comfortable German.

Although, Daniel looked no different than the bulk of the Polish slave laborers still awash in Germany, we struck up an instant rapport.

Within a day, I understood why. He was in reality a survivor of the notorious death camp, Buchenwald. As I, he was Jewish.

I have never been able to understand this mystical connection. In my later travels about the world, this experience would be duplicated again and again, even among those separated by continents who had made every effort to "pass" into the larger society. Wherever it is geographically, Jewish people seem to be magnetically drawn to a recognition of each other.

I don't know whether it is in the genes, or in the culture, but there is a certain softer, forgiving nature, an almost sadly humorous acceptance of the world condition, that binds the spirits.

In short, he was the spark that illuminated this dreary station and was well liked, especially by the cooks with whom he had established a nurturing umbilical chord connection.

In retrospect, having later learned more about the death camps, and considering that he was the only survivor of his family, I was amazed at Daniel's lack of outward hatred and bitterness toward the German people. He seemed to accept the Holocaust as only the most recent manifestation of an historical phenomena, in which only the nationality of the practitioner had rotated.

He had fattened up somewhat on Army chow but his generally healthy condition indicated to me later that as a survivor he had been one of the younger boys in the Camp, who had served the Master in more ways than one.

Like the US Army guys, he felt obligated to reward the local willing Frauleins and their families from the copious supplies of the US army, a horn of plenty whose tip stretched back into the pockets of the U. S. taxpayer.

The second evening, I went along with him to make delivery to a small cottage several blocks away. We mounted the wooden stairs to the small apartment above.

There in a rocking chair sat Grandmother, rocking and knitting and three young granddaughters in their late teens sitting on the couch.

Daniel chatted with them for a short time and then went off to the kitchen with one to store the provisions.

Meanwhile, I sat silently, rather uncomfortable with this typical German farm family, devoid of the males lost during the long years of the war.

The girls did everything to make me feel at home. They smiled at me shyly, even coyly, with their half turned heads. I was rather flattered by their attention, and I was thinking, I must have unknowingly filled out and become quite attractive during my combat maturing.

It seemed a hell of a long time before Daniel returned, and after a few more pleasantries, we left.

As we walked down the middle of the moon lighted street, after some hesitation, Daniel asked me whether I liked girls.

"Of course I like girls!"

"Then, why didn't you make love with one of them?"

"In front of their Grandmother?"

Daniel stopped dead and looked at me. "Das war einen Katzenhaus!"

"Einen Katzenhouse? A cat house?" Recognition dawned. That was no typical bucolic German family. That was no Grandmother. That was a whorehouse and she was the madam.

I grabbed Daniel's arm: "Let's go back!"

THE IMMORTAL ARCHWAY

There is probably no one who has seen an illustrated calendar, who would not recognize the famous clock archway through a building in the old Bavarian town of Rothenberg.

Every time I see such a photo, I shudder, because it reminds me of the time I almost slaughtered a platoon of innocent German pedestrians walking through it.

When I arrived at the H.Q. of the ambulance company on an elevation outside of the town, I was aquiver with the excitement I have written about in a previous chapter. I was going, at last, to see some of the mothers of our western culture, the famous towns of Europe.

The problem was that I had never learned to drive, that is, I knew how, but had never actually done it. In those days, dads didn't give up the treasured family buses to wanton adolescent destruction.

I was not going to be deterred! Detroit told me, all you had to do is remember to double clutch when you shifted.

Sgt. Gorski, a very unsympathetic Polish-American type from the near North Side of Chicago was going to test and qualify me the next morning. The fact that we were fellow burghers from Chicago didn't seem to make much difference.

That evening, I snuck down to the motor pool below our house and started up one of the ambulances and practiced shifting and moving slowly around the area. Then I thought, "What the Hell!" and I swung out onto the road going down the hill.

That wasn't too bad, because I had steered before, sitting on my daddy's lap. But then I needed to turn around, and I promptly back-ended into one of those ubiquitous ditches that border the narrow roads of Bavaria. My headlights were streaking into the sky like kleig lights searching for enemy aircraft.

Thank God for four wheel drive! I was able to get out. But, I did gratuitously create a 45 degree angle feeder culvert for the Germans in doing so.

The next morning was the "Moment of truth!" Freedom for Don Quixote to adventure abroad or be returned to the routine humdrum of our company aid station.

I made it up the hill to the door of our H.Q. without going over the edge and luckily my struggle to turn around was not witnessed by Sgt. Gorski before he emerged at 10:00 AM.

He got in and searched my face: "Are you sure you know how to drive?"

"I'm an old hand, Sarge!"

As I said, steering down the hill was no problem.

Half way down he asked: "Don't you think you ought to start the engine now?"

"Just saving gas for Uncle Sam, Sarge!"

At the bottom of the hill we rolled to a stop. The ambulance started all right, but, when I forgot to double clutch, it screamed in pain as I tried to shift into first.

Gorski was bending over and looking into my face, shaking his head almost imperceptibly.

"Sorry, Sarge!" I got it into gear and began turning onto the road going away from town that I had explored the previous evening. Gorski grabbed my arm.

"No! Up through the town."

"Through the town?" He nodded, yes.

I shrieked into reverse after exploring 2nd and 4th gears first, and then wheeled to the left and began the ascent.

I was really quite pleased. I was holding the road well in climbing gears and we entered through the town gates and drove through the busy streets.

Then, I saw the famous clock tower arch approaching. I tried to slow down. "Pick it up!" said Gorski and I did. My foot clamped down on the accelerator hard and our heads were throw back like climbing fighter pilots.

I couldn't see the faces, but the bodies in front of us demonstrated horror.

There was a scattering, as if an unexploded shell had just landed in the middle of the Strasse.

The people in the archway were flattening portly bodies against the walls.

As we sped through, I was praying that those thumps I was hearing against the sides of the ambulance were walls and not flattened ham burghers.

We were emerging from the other side and through the gate entering the plateau, when Gorski screamed: "Stop!"

He got out of the ambulance, and walked around it searching for blood. He got back in and asked: "Do you think you can do better on this straight open road ahead?"

I was hurt. I thought I had done quite well on that first leg of the test. No casualties yet!

To call these "roads" was an exaggeration. They dated back to the days when the only transportation was by horseback riders and farm wagons, so as a matter of fact, they were only an American-style lane and a half from side to side, with the inevitable ditches bordering, of course.

Have you ever noticed how narrow and agile Bavarian Motors cars are? That's because with modern vehicles, the Bavarians have established a civility that mandates that one slow up, even have wheels leave the road, in order to pass safely.

But, I was an American, with a big-assed ambulance!

Approaching me on the proper side of the road was an old farmer behind a wooden-staked farm wagon being drawn by a placid ox. Behind him trotted a bunch of his geese. They politely began edging off the side of the road.

But, I was accustomed to wide American lanes, so I was barrelling straight down the middle. "Pull over! Pull over!" Gorski was shouting as he cringed and covered his eyes.

I heard this crash at the left side and heard geese honking "Howdy's" to us as we passed.

I looked into the side mirror and said, "That's interesting. That ox just went down into the ditch to drink."

Gorski uncovered his eyes and looked back over his shoulder: "Private! Stop! Turn around! Go back!"

I obeyed. I stopped, did a three point turn around with tires so close to the edge each time that Gorski was looking down at the abyss below. Then, I straighten out and took off for home.

The road was absolutely clear now. As we passed him in the ditch, the old farmer waved his staff at us screaming German obscenities. I don't know what the geese were saying.

Strangely, the clock archway was abandoned when we went back the other way, and soon I pulled up at the H.Q. door.

In those days before seat belts, Gorski's knuckles were white from grasping the door handle. He sat looking at me and shaking his head a bit.

"Private, I don't know whether you are the greatest driver I have ever tested or whether you are America's revenge upon the Germans. I am going to pass you."

Well, then again, the U.S. Army never did have very high standards.

ABORTED ORGASM

Fortune finally favored me!

I had a job I literally adored: ambulance pick-ups all over Western Europe. It was an artist's fantasy: Paris! Amsterdam! Brussels! Lyon! Venice! Florence! Rome!

What matter that I didn't really know how to drive!

What matter that they wouldn't let me drive through the clock arch in Rothenberg again!

I was free! ---- That is until the Major called me in the next day.

"General Patch wants a personal band for the Seventh Army Command in Heidelberg. They dug up your M.O. as a musician. You're transferred."

"No! I won't go!"

"What do you mean, you won't go?"

"When I wanted to play a musical instrument, they gave me a 57 MM cannon. Now, when I want to drive an ambulance, they give me a musical instrument."

"Well, here's your transfer. Go tell, General Patch, yourself."

Never had I been so depressed. From the heights to the pits.

This curse followed me through my entire stay in the Army. I was 32nd of 36 in the lottery for Paris. Every time I was about to be promoted, I was transferred. Now, this! I was almost a Kamikaze victim getting this damn job!

It was almost enough to make me mad at God, again!

THE PITS

It wasn't until I joined the newly formed band that I came to know how deep that pit really was.

In this converted fraternity house on the campus of Heidelberg University was gathered a gaggle of pot-smoking, drug taking, alcoholic jazz band musicians, three church musicians and me.

The first sergeant in charge was a regular Army, yes I said regular Army clarinetist, who was more chicken-shit than Sergeant Archer at his worst.

It was this man's absolute obsession that we all be out of bed at 6:00 AM reveille, which was absolutely against my personal religion.

This was a collision course.

His "hidden agenda" was based upon the fact that this was the last opportunity he could foresee to leave the enlisted ranks and join the officers as a warrant officer in charge of the band.

His "modus operandi" was:

1. Develop clout with the Chief of Special Services at 7th Army H.Q.

He did!

2. Selflessly, get an R&R rotation home for the current Warrant officer.

He did!

3. Block him from returning to Heidelberg.

Which he did!

4. Have a cracker jack unit.

Which he didn't!

So that was his challenge and I, this noble, bemedalled, and beribboned warrior, was again on shit details.

Added to the heaping indignities was the fact that, frozen in rank by refusing to reenlist, we, the combat veterans, were now being superseded in rank by downy-cheeked eighteen-year-old newcomers.

Then, a tragic setback for the first sergeant! His clout at Seventh Army H.Q. was bumped to make way for the son of a General at 3rd Corps.

He needed to start all over again.

The sergeant ass-kissed the new guy to come over and inspect our quarters, and it became my job to make the hallways and latrines immaculate.

There I was in my undershorts, making like Cinderella, scrubbing the stairs, when who should the sergeant bring in but my old combat buddy, Lt. "West Point," who is now a Major!

"Attention!" cried the Sergeant.

Instead of attention, what he got was an immaculately pressed officer and a skinny private in undershorts, combat blood brothers both, in a crushing embrace.

"Attention!" he yelled.

We sat down on the stairs.

"Attention!" he screamed.

"Get to hell out of here, will you!" said the Major as he turned to me to discuss "old times."

That very evening, another sergeant who was second command of the band was moved out of his private room on the top floor of the fraternity house to my bunk in the barracks, while a special detail of band members moved me and my German Shepherd dog into his private room.

It pays to have friends in high places.

Rudolph, the Cold-Nosed Shepherd

I mentioned my dog.

To me, a dog had always meant a German Shepherd dog, and the beauty of all dogdom was matched to that standard.

So when this Headquarters guy who was being shipped stateside offered me "Rudolph," I was quivering with anticipation.

Most guys tried to sneak their pets home on the ship under their shirts, but it would have been difficult with Rudolph.. He weighed 50 pounds.

The advantage and disadvantage with Rudolph, who was a year old when I got him, was that from birth to about 4 months, he had been raised by a German family and spoken to in German only. When this German-American G. I. got him, he decided to carry on the commands in German to control the dog more privately. I decided to continue the tradition.

The disadvantage was, that no one else could handle him for me when I was out and the Sergeant was blowing blood vessels.

He would be yelling such things as "Attention! Attention!" at him and Rudolph would be sitting on his haunches, head cocked, ignoring him with a face of Teutonic indifference.

Anyone who walked him for me was a prisoner of Germany. Since, Rudolph did not understand English, I taught the guys some simple commands like "Sit", which is "Setz" in German. If they didn't pronounce it just right, it converted in Rudolph's brain to "shpritz" (spray) so to the dismay of the dog sitter, he might have a wet pants leg.

In other words, a Rin-tin-tin he was not, but it was un-American not to love a dog, so he got lots of affection all over the place.

What he lacked in brain power, he made up for in pure loyalty -- to my room.

It was his interpretation of loyalty that his mission was to protect my room, even from me.

The Sergeant could never come in to inspect.

That was good!

I could never come in unless Rudolph inspected me.

That was bad!

His eyes were not good, so he relied mostly on his sense of smell. So there I would be, plastered against the door jamb with Rudolph's heavy paws on my chest while he gave me the old nose examination from head to toe, with unpleasant special attention to the middle.

You could imagine what a special thrill this was when I was returning from the shower!

I would later come to think of him as "Rudolph, the Cold Nosed Shepherd."

The worst time was the one and only rip-snortin' drunk I have ever had in my life. I was taking some studies at Heidelberg University and one night after classes the German students were teaching me student drinking songs at the local bier stube.

The only problem was, one had to down a drink after each song. By the 20th "down," the boys were leading my home by my leash.

Rudolph wouldn't let me come into the room! All he could smell, even at my "special" middle, were liquor fumes.

"Please Rudolph!" over and over, but Rudolph was playing Horatio at the bridge. "They shall not pass!"

I fell asleep in the hallway.

Of all things, Rudolph was afraid of mice, and we had one that would sneak into my room through the door to the attic. Rudolph would sit cowering in the corner, howling.

It was the howling, not compassion, that brought all the others jamming into my small room while I was in bed.

While I hid under the covers and Rudolph cowered, they were racing around the room and stepping on my body as they were swinging brooms and rolled up Stars and Stripes newspapers at the little thing.

I am sure the mouse really died of fright.

I am also sure that being owned by Rudolph is what made me a dedicated cat lover after returning to the States.

FIBBER McGEE'S CLOSET

Black marketing was achieved as a big, medium, or small business.

Big business was Lt. Collins, my affable Southern gentleman friend, who enlisted me as his interpreter with promises of a payoff in the States until I nauseated myself out of his service three days later.

Medium business was Corporal Gottfried, a good looking, very smooth and pleasant German-American, very fluent in his family's mother tongue, who was one of the sober fellow members of the General's Band.

He began shacking with his Fraulein even before fraternization prohibition was lifted and, consequently, never slept in our fraternity house dorm. The First Sergeant couldn't make a fuss about this, because he was shacking, too.

I would see him about town in civilian clothes looking very native. He would wave, pleasantly, and move off about his business.

What his business was, I found out later, was laundering black market money into valuable properties in Heidelberg, which zoomed in value as the Seventh Army headquarters grew and more staff was pouring in from the United States. At that time, his net worth was in the hundreds of thousands of dollars, millions by today's standards.

Small time business were two Brooklyn boys in our band. They were a kind of Abbott and Costello combination, with Abbott, a slouched figure, turning his body slowly at 45 degree angles with each step, hands crammed in his pockets playing with his "jollies."

Costello, was a lovable chubby shadow upon whom he would regularly take out his frustrations.

Abbott would slouch up and, standing next to us, speak softly "movie style" out of the corner of his mouth: "Wanna sell some cigarettes?"

It was a good deal for the buyer and the seller. For the seller, if he wasn't a smoker, he could get seven and a half dollars for his weekly allotment and Abbott could wholesale it out for maybe fifteen dollars.

But to all, even the pot-smoking dissipates, there was a distaste for these two.

We had full length wooden lockers in our dorm room. Number 8 was called "Fibber McGee's Closet" like the famous one in the radio show that poured out onto Fibber McGee.

The First Sergeant had this disgusting habit of coming into the dorm, talking to us, and then without warning, turning quickly to open one of our lockers for a quick inspection.

So, we loaded up number 8 with every bit of paraphernalia we could find loose around the fraternity house, including a boar's head souvenir from a 1898 hunt.

There was a duffle bag with fifty pounds of junk, brooms, mops, buckets, even some ball bearings someone had brought in from the motor pool.

Every time the sergeant came in after that, we would lie on our bunks in baited anticipation. But he always missed it! He opened to the right of it. He opened to the left of it.

Never it!

We were all lying there mad as hell, when Abbott and Costello came in. We were silent. Hands deep in pockets, Abbott slouch-stepped to the middle of the room with Costello closely following and then did a sharp pivot to face us.

"Anyone got any cigarettes to sell?" he whispered out of the corner of his mouth.

We all lay there silently for a moment. Then, Sgt. Neeley said: "Yah! They're over there in locker 8."

He pivoted, slouched to locker 8, pivoted to look at us again and reached out from his right side to pull open the locker door.

All hell fell out past him, culminating with the ball bearing rolling slowly across the floor.

He stood there without a change of expression: "Very funny! Very funny!" Then, he punched Costello and walked out.

We reloaded the booby trap locker for the First Sergeant again.

I wish there was a happier ending to this story.

One day, I was alone in the house with three cleaning ladies and was taking a shower. I couldn't find any soap, so I went dripping wet and freezing into the dorm pulling open locker after locker.

I forgot about locker number 8. Out fell a fifty pound duffle bag, brooms, mops, boar's head and all the rest of "Fibber McGee's" closet. I stood there stunned! I can still hear the ball bearing rolling slowly across the floor.

Then, I heard three female voices behind me: "Vas ist los!" "Vas ist los!"

I turned.

Now, I know that European women are very accustomed to seeing naked men, but I wasn't about to join that culture.

I must have looked very macho with those boar's tusks growling at them from my middle while I was clutching a fifty pound duffel bag to my bosom!

FLASHBACKS

All organisms react to shocks differently.

I usually cry and grieve immediately, and don't repress the memory. I am lucky.

Some internalize, and have the event chew up their insides until the damage is too great to repair.

Some go into denial, only to have the event come back upon the screen of their mind with tube shattering violence.

The first psychological breakdown we had in the Seventh Army Band was Jansen, our snare drummer. He was a blonde, slim, clean cut, good looking guy, which was a rarity in our slovenly outfit.

I could see from the trembling in his body, the look in his eyes, and the infrequency of his speech that there was something going on in there.

When I first joined the band, he and I had adjoining single rooms at the back of the fraternity house. I had a window which looked up at the famous old Heidelberg Schloss (Castle) atop the small mountain beyond. There was only forest mounting to the heights.

One night, some yowling cat got into that forest and the echoes made the atmosphere, with the moon shining through the vacant castle windows, seem like a scene out of a Dracula movie.

At a about 3:00 AM I was conscious of Jansen standing fully dressed at my window, moonlight illuminating his face. The yowling was still intense.

I got up and went over to his side. He was no longer trembling and his face was placidly looking out at nothing.

I recognized the Sgt. Wagner syndrome.

I led him back to his bed and pulled a blanket over him.

In the morning, Sgt. Williams drove him to the Seventh Army medical center.

They came over later for his things. He never returned.

I said to Williams: "It is horrible what combat does to some guys!"

"Combat? He wasn't in combat. He's strung out on drugs."

Only then, did I find out what those funny smelling "roll- your-owns" being passed around at the jazz band rehearsals were. If you can believe it, I was baritone sax man on our Armed Forces Radio Saturday night jazz band programs.

It also explained some of the other things the guys were passing around that made me feel like an outsider. After that, I preferred to remain an outsider.

Also, it ended my inclination to be a psychiatric diagnostician, until Sgt. Madigan.

Madigan, our trombone player, had been a combat veteran who turned to heavy drinking to drown out the memories.

Each night after dinner, he disappeared into the beer stubes of Heidelberg and didn't reappear at his first floor dorm room until the wee hours.

The guys decided to play a practical joke on him. Understandable! Our lives had degenerated into a boredom that I was able to relieve only by attending classes at the University of Heidelberg.

The first two nights in succession, someone slept in his bed, so that when he came in, he had to roust them.

The third night, they sprang the trap. They put his full duffel bag under the blanket and mounted our famous boar's head, tusks and all, at the head. Then they pulled up the blanket.

At about 2:00 AM someone shook me in my third floor bunk. "You're a medic. There is something wrong with Madigan."

I raced down the two flights. There stood Madigan, body rigid, looking down upon the boar's head with a Sgt. Wagner look on his face.

This time, it was the real thing.

In the morning the medics picked him and his equipment up.

I was really pissed off: "Will you guys cut this crap out and stick to short-sheeting beds?"

They promised they would and they kept their promise.

The next night, I sprained all my toes slipping under the covers.

TIT FOR TAT

One day, I realized that in selling my cigarettes to Abbott and Costello, I had accumulated many more Marks than I could spend in Germany before I would be going home.

"Why don't you buy something valuable here and sell it at home for dollars," they suggested.

The idea really didn't appeal to me, especially since it had come from them.

But, small-bore greed overcame me and when I spotted a beautiful jeweled ring featured in the window of a shop on the main street of Heidelberg, I walked in to inquire about the price.

"This is only for German people to buy," said one of the men behind the glass-topped counter.

"What do you mean?"

"You Americans are buying up everything with your money. There is nothing left for the people of our country."

I was really getting mad! After all, who had won the war that they had started?

Seeing how angry I had become, the owner pulled the ring out of it's honored place in the show window and plunked it down on the counter.

He gave me the price. It ate up just about all of the excess Marks that I had, but it was worth it. No German was going to push me around.

I went out thinking, well at least I can get my dough back home.

I hid my little "nest egg" in my pack. I looked at the stone every so often and grudgingly mentally thanked Abbott and Costello.

When I was back in Chicago, I went down to jewelry row on Clark street and placed the little gem in its box onto the counter.

"How much?"

He took it out of the box and looked at it through his glass.

"I'll give you two bucks"

"What?"

"Well, that's all that German silver is worth!"

"That's a precious stone in there! I paid over three hundred bucks in German money for that!"

He put his magnifying lens over his eye again.

"Sir! This is a piece of colored glass!"

I was stunned. I stood looking at him. Then, I collapsed in laughter and staggered out of the door onto Clark Street.

"Sir! Your ring."

I waved him off: "Keep it!"

How could I tell him, I got what I deserved. I'll never be a good crook. I'm too dumb.

I tried to get the Germans and they got me.

It was tit for tat.

OLD SOLDIERS DO DIE

In early December, General Patton was involved in an automobile accident several blocks from our fraternity house billet. Rumor was that he was drunk and with his girlfriend.

The event aroused great indifference among the troops. He did not represent the same humane image as our own General Patch of the Seventh Army or General Bradley of the Third Corps.

Our division being the furthest north of the Seventh Army we had to struggle to maintain contact with the southern most division of Patton's hard-driven Third Army. I never spoke with a Third Army man who liked him.

He died, unlamented, several weeks later in our Heidelberg base hospital.

HEILIGEN NACHT

On Christmas Eve, 1945, I sang "Silent Night" in the Old Church of Heidelberg.

It's an undistinguished Baroque structure standing in the center of the old town.

Sgt. Bud Neeley, another combat veteran, was one of the church musicians in our Seventh Army band. He had organized and trained a church choir of German civilians and American soldiers, but needed someone to solo this concluding number in the services in German, so he asked me.

The services were conducted by the head chaplain of the Seventh Army, a Catholic, a German-American and a Colonel.

The sermon was one of the most memorable I have ever heard.

First, he reviewed the importance of Christ as the Prince of Peace. Then in a slowly rising pitch of anger he asked them, if they were here to worship the essence of the religion founded upon that teaching, how they could have participated in, or stood by silently while that teaching was violated in the worst orgy of hatred in the recorded history of mankind.

When he concluded, there were audible sobs in the congregation.

Then, there was dead silence.

In the loft, Bud cued me to start.

With the choir humming behind me, I stood at the front of the loft and started:

"Stille nacht! Heiligen nacht! Alles schlaft, einsam wacht........"

I wasn't even thinking of the words anymore. I had heard that same carol sung in two languages on the battle field exactly one year ago that night.

I was lifting my voice in a way I had never sung before and never have again. All of my studies in the great humane music of Western Civilization poured into those brief moments and with great clarity the carol was filling every nook and cranny of that ancient structure.

There was a force focusing from outside of me, surpassing any specific theological creed. It was like an ecumenical voice of hope in a world of despair.

Bud was no longer conducting. He was looking at me strangely. The Chaplain was looking up and the congregation was turning in their pews.

Then, across my mind flashed the horrors of even that small bit of despair that I had witnessed, and by the time I had reached the end of the carol,

"Schlaf in himmlischer Ruhe. Schlaf..."

I was realizing how savagely the message of the Prince of Peace had been violated, my voice broke on the last words and there were tears streaming down my face.

If this God is a good God how could He have permitted mankind's worst self administered catastrophe to have occurred?

Dead, twenty-five million Russians, six million Jews, millions upon millions of Germans, French, English, Japanese, and others. Many more millions maimed. To this day, I've never found an answer to this question.

"FRONT AND CENTER!"

By March, 1946, the routine of the Seventh Army Headquarters having become boring, West Point, now a Lt. Colonel, scheduled an awards ceremony for those of the remaining combat veterans who had been awarded but had not yet given their combat decorations.

Our band led the troops onto the field, playing "The Army Caisson March" until we were in a straight line across the parade ground.

"Right face!" Heels clicked.

West Point and the Commanding General were driven onto the field in a jeep and disembarked.

Our boys played a trumpet salute.

The General saluted.

"Awardees, front and center!" West Point was at his best!

Beside me, there were Bud Neeley and Gottfried from the band among the awardees. We about faced, right faced, walked behind the first line, halted and right faced.

"Awardees, forward harch!" We snapped bones.

"Hup, tup, threep, fup, hup, tup, threep fup, Awardees, halt, hup, tup!"

There were about thirty of us in all. The General, followed by West Point, walked down the line from our right, going through a short ceremony and pinning on the medals at each soldier.

When he reached me, West Point called out "Four steps forward, harch!"

Hup, tup, threep, halt!

"Hand salute!" I snapped up so hard, I almost poked my eye out.

The General returned the salute, stepped forward and pinned on the medal with two oak leaf clusters.

He shook my hand. "Good work, soldier!"

"Thank you, Sir!"

West Point smiled and winked at me. From a combat mate, that meant much more than the medals.

I took one step backward and saluted.

Then, about face, hup, tup, threep, halt, about face, hup, halt! I was back in line.

Our band led the detachment off of the field with John Phillip Sousa's, "Stars and Stripes, Forever!"

This was the last time, commencing with my first ROTC year in high school, that I was to march the parade grounds. There was a deep pang in my middle.

That this pacifist should take such pride in membership in the United States Army Infantry only demonstrates the paradoxical diversities in our human natures.

Like most others, I wasn't champing at the bit to serve, but, if called, I didn't resist or regret.

When called, I was exactly where I wanted to be, in the Army, not the Navy, Marines, or Coast Guard.

When in the Army, not in supply, transport or other support services but in the Infantry, which is after all, the real purpose for the organization's existence.

And, if in a combat area, on the line.

That was the rub! The possibility of me shooting, bayoneting or hurting someone, except in self-defense, was too remote to register on any scale.

So God, fate or chance put me exactly where I should have been, in the greatest danger, helping, not hurting.

In that respect only, life had been good.

To those who look down upon the riflemen as a "grunt" or "dogface," or whatever, too stupid not to have landed a cushier post, I bear witness that they are the cream of the crop. Death occurs everywhere, in the air, aboard ships, but never as dirty as in ground combat.

They march and move through fear, daily. A few break down. A very few run. But on the whole, most served because they were asked to, and if they survived, returned to the same repressive social, racial, religious and economic pecking orders from whence they emerged, while the barracks and marching field heroes reemerged from their shadows:

"Front and Center!"

I still hadn't seen any of the great cities of Europe, but I was ready to go home.

YOU MUST GO HOME AGAIN

The Greek philosopher Plato wrote the parable of the cave, where inhabitants were chained so they could see only the shadows of what was occurring outside. When someone escaped and then returned they were unable to communicate the truth to the others.

I felt that way after I returned home.

How could I explain war to "gung ho" John Wayne types?

How should I respond to one who is ecstatic at how he profited financially during the war years, and says: "If only it had lasted a little longer....." The most painful losses were those who died in the last days and hours of the conflict.

I remembered that after World War I, American Legion and Veterans of Foreign Wars were big things, and they probably still are.

I can understand why. Their members are the only ones who can really communicate with each other regarding their experiences.

Because I considered serving only as an interruption of my normal life, I never joined a veteran's organization nor ever used such service as a political or social qualification, as so many veterans shamelessly did in the post WW II days.

Actually, what I did return to was the same social, economic, religious and family pecking orders that I had left.

So, I really didn't miss anything.

PARTING IS SUCH SWEET SORROW

It's Camp McCoy, Wisconsin, April, 1946. We are doing our final processing for discharge.

I walk into the mess hall for chow.

I'm intercepted by this sergeant and this corporal who look like they posed for one of those U. S. Army recruiting brochures. They are very clean cut, handsome, smiling, and pleasant. I don't remember seeing this type too often in the fighting Army.

"We are here to serve you, Soldier!"

"Thanks! I can manage for myself."

The sergeant takes me by the arm: "I see by your ribbons that you are one of our boys who really served. Please, be our guest!"

He leads me to a special table at the side. He sits down opposite me. I'm sort of embarrassed.

While we wait, he admires my medals and ribbons and I have to give him a rundown on how I got them, and where I served and all that usual crap. Actually, I am really hungry.

The corporal finally brings this tray full of knockout food. It looks like it's out of Henrici's, the famous restaurant in Chicago. Steak, dripping with juice, baked potatoes with all of the works, green vegetables, and just about everything I love and had not had since I had been in the Army.

He puts it down in front of the sergeant. I'm salivating like a Boston bull dog. Boy! The Army sure knows how to show gratitude to combat veterans!

The sergeant pushes the tray slowly across the table to me.

I take the silverware off the tray and am about to plunge in.

"While you are eating, I would like to discuss with you the benefits of serving in the U. S. Army Reserves."

I look up at him.

Our eyes lock for a moment.

I push the tray back across the table to him, and get up.

I go to the chow line.
The mess sergeant looks up.
"What's for lunch, Sarge?"